Praise for *LIGHT*

"In this beautifully written, insightful, and courageous book, Nancy Levine has given us a story of her family's struggle with anorexia. As a memoir, it's an engaging read, a window into the lives of interesting people as they cope with a dangerous illness. But more than that, this is an important book. Anyone dealing with anorexia, as a patient, family member, or helper, will find hope and inspiration in its pages. As a therapist working with couples and families, I highly recommend it. Five stars!"

—Dr. Bruce Chalmer, author of *Betrayal and Forgiveness: How to Navigate the Turmoil and Learn to Trust Again*

"Nancy Levine's memoir, *Light*, tells the story of a family in a battle with their daughter's anorexia. Including passages written by her daughter, Rachel Levine-Spates, this book is ultimately about the way our choices can influence our children. It's a story of abiding love, told in the most direct terms and with the desire to know the intricate ties that bind even when illness threatens to sever them. I rooted for this family, and I know you will, too. This is a beautifully written book, a book of sacrifice and survival and one that will touch you in the most important ways."

—Lee Martin, author of the *The Bright Forever*, a finalist for the 2006 Pulitzer Prize in Fiction

"Heartache, to promise, to triumph, to joy! This book is a must-read for everyone who knows anyone struggling with an eating disorder, and for everyone who is struggling with an eating disorder themselves. The story is masterfully told by Nancy Levine with the deep love of a mom who watched her daughter face the agony and devastation of an eating disorder, recover with the support and love of her family and others, and blossom into a beautiful woman with a wonderful family of her own. When someone we love suffers from an eating disorder it can become hard to hold on to hope. This heartfelt, warm and honest book brings encouragement and inspiration that recovery is possible!"

—Dr. Lorraine Platka-Bird, registered dietitian, certified eating disorder specialist, and certified diabetes educator

Light

A Mother and Daughter Memoir of Anorexia

by Nancy Levine
with Rachel Levine-Spates

Montpelier, VT

Light: A Mother and Daughter Memoir of Anorexia ©2024

Release Date: August 26, 2025

All Rights Reserved.

Printed in the USA.

Paperback ISBN: 978-1-57869-206-4
eBook ISBN: 978-1-57869-207-1

Library of Congress Control Number: 2025909649

Published by Rootstock Publishing
an imprint of Ziggy Media, LLC
Montpelier, VT 05602

info@rootstockpublishing.com
www.rootstockpublishing.com

Book Design by Eddie Vincent, ENC Graphic Services.

Ornamental section divider designed by Freepik (www.freepik.com).

Book Cover Photograph by Megan Humphrey, "Lovely Lake Light" ©2025, https://www.etsy.com/shop/SweetBasilCards. Used by permission of the artist.

"Love After Love" poem by Derek Walcott, originally from *Collected Poems 1948-1984* by Derek Walcott. Copyright ©1986. Reprinted by the permission of Faber and Faber Ltd., The Bindery, 51 Hatton Garden, London EC1N 8HN.

Nancy Y. Levine author photo by Karen Pike.

Rachel Levine-Spates author photo by Jamison Photography.

The stories in this book reflect the author's recollection of events. Some names, locations, and identifying characteristics have been changed to protect the privacy of those depicted. Dialogue has been re-created from memory.

No AI training; no part of this book may be reproduced or transmitted in any form or by any means, electronic or mechanical, including photocopying, recording, or by an information storage and retrieval system (except by a journalist or reviewer who may quote brief passages in an academic or editorial review) without permission in writing.

For reprint permissions, or to schedule a book club visit or author reading, contact Nancy at nlevine35@gmail.com.

Light

For Mark

"Maybe you have to know the darkness before you can appreciate the light."
—Madeleine L'Engle, *A Ring of Endless Light*

Author's Note

I am indebted to my daughter, Rachel Levine-Spates, for editing this memoir and allowing me to tell her story. This work we did together was the privilege of a lifetime. I thank her for sharing her journals, the poisonous voice of her eating disorder, and for writing the Afterword. The journal notations appear in italics at the end of some chapters. The eating disorder voice also appears in italics at the end of some chapters. The names of nonfamily members have been changed. All places and all times are accurate, as recollected. Both Rachel and I have drawn from journals, letters, and calendars in our writing. It would be impossible to recreate conversations word for word, but we have done the best we could and feel they represent what was said. It was important to us that we did not conflate characters or scenes to better present the story. This is how it happened.

—Nancy Levine, April 2025

Prologue

Nevada, 2007

Pink roses cascade down a split-rail fence bordering a pigpen on the outskirts of Reno. Orson, the pot-bellied pig within, is blind. His pudgy legs are crippled by arthritis and his stomach sweeps the ground as he follows my daughter's voice to his steel food dish. I'm digging my fingernails into the palm of my hand so I won't cry as I watch them.

Rachel is twenty-three and five foot eleven inches. In the past year she's lost all her muscle, all her subcutaneous fat, all her former health. On this blistering hot July day, she's wearing khaki shorts and a white tank top. A network of prominent veins traverses her ravaged body and I'm in awe that one so physically depleted can stand in the merciless sun and cajole a pig, who looks in even worse shape, to eat.

"C'mon baby," she croons. "Just a little further. I know you can do it."

This is the same engaging voice I heard when I volunteered in the first-grade class Rachel taught. Like those kids, Orson responds to her. He plods to his dish, lowers his head, sniffs the food as if suspect, then chows down his meal.

"Orson is, you know, O-B-E-S-E," Rachel says with a wicked grin. "We aren't allowed to use words like that here. Kind of weird that he's here, isn't it?"

"Sure is," I agree.

"Kind of weird that I'm here, too; I bet you never thought you'd see me in a place like this."

"Never in a million years." My voice cracks. I think, no, I never saw you of all people winding up in an eating disorders treatment center. Especially one with an ailing pig who'd been grandfathered into the contract when the Center for Hope bought this place.

Rachel and I laugh—it's tentative but if roses bloom here maybe laughter can too. I think someone, maybe God, or perhaps the goddess of fate, laughed even harder and then tossed one bizarre metaphor our way. A pig living in an eating disorders center, one who must be coerced to eat by a girl so thin that she's nearly transparent. A girl who must also be forced to eat because a voice only she hears screams that she's the pig.

I watch Rachel with an unsettling mix of disbelief and gutting reality. Once a shiny mass of brown waves rippled down her freckled back; now her hair is dull and wispy and, like Orson's, as brittle as sunburnt straw.

"I'm glad you have him," I say. "When you were little, you always wanted a pet pig. Here he is."

"Well no one else wanted to take care of him. So I'm doing it all the time."

"I'm not surprised," I tell her. Since childhood Rachel has been a caretaker, first of her dolls, then her friends, later the children she babysat for, and eventually, the students she taught in AmeriCorps. "I'm incredibly proud of you for being here."

She smiles through quivering lips and I know that at this moment, my words carry weight.

"This is hell," I continue. "But there's nothing you could be doing now that's more important than getting healthy. You will get better. I promise."

I promise wellness, but knowing how anorexia damages a heart, alters kidney and liver function, causes osteoporosis, affects brain neurochemistry, and for one in ten is fatal, my promise is a sacred vow. How can she recover if I doubt her ability to do so? If she senses my fear, she'll absorb it as hers.

The novelist Ann Hood writes, "I have learned that there is more power in a good strong hug than in a thousand meaningful words." Clinging to one another, my hug conveys all those words of sorrow as I have watched Rachel waste away, for that is what anorexia is, a wasting of body, of soul, of hope. Her hug, followed by a well of tears, says I'm sorry over and over and over.

As the blasted sun scorches us, I long for our cool, verdant Vermont and how good life was before anorexia blindsided us. Yes, I never guessed that Rachel would end up in a place like this but here she is.

Maybe this inexorable trip to Reno began at Rachel's conception, when roughly twenty-four thousand genes tumbled the double helix of chromosomes that led nine months later to our beloved wide-eyed baby girl. When I put her to my breast that first time, I simply admired how she latched on and ate like a champ. Little did I know back then that genes could contribute to a 50-80 percent risk for anorexia or bulimia.[1]

And at that wondrous moment, why even consider such a thing?

Or perhaps that inexorable trip began on an Australian beach twenty-one years later. At least, that's where we thought it did. But like many stories, there are multiple beginnings. The ones we are aware of, but also the ones lost in the hidden gullies of memory.

Chapter One

Australia, 2005

The Benadryl I'd taken for sleep worked for the first ninety minutes of a fifteen-hour flight from Los Angeles to Sydney. Crunched between my husband, Mark, and a snoring man about twice my size, I woke with cramped legs and settled in for a long chain of forgettable movies. Foraging on peanuts, pretzels, and chips, I landed the next day with ankles like water balloons. It was 8 a.m. Australia time, 3 p.m. California time, but my internal clock ticked in Vermont. I wasn't jet-lagged; I was jet-dragged as I limped off the plane into the Technicolor Australian morning.

Still, I was thrilled. As a kid, I hadn't traveled far from my upstate New York home. My family and friends weren't the passport kind of people so I didn't miss something others had. However, by college I yearned to see the world, even if through the grimy windows of the Greyhound bus taking me from Ithaca to school in Pittsburgh. The more distant world came into focus after graduation. As a nurse, I worked hard but played just as hard on vacations. Adrenalin flowed as I stuffed a suitcase, figured out my destination on a Triple A map, or better yet, boarded a plane.

I met my husband Mark at a Halloween party when I was twenty-seven. There I was, a grown Irish-Catholic woman, often working as a charge nurse in a neonatal intensive care unit, quickly falling for a younger Jewish medical student with a big smile and a wild Jewfro. We had almost everything in common except religion. We knew that would take time to figure out. It certainly did and three years later we were married by both a priest and a rabbi. We looked forward to a family, and better yet, traveling with our future kids who turned out to be Mike and Rachel.

Born two-and-a-half years apart, they squabbled like magpies at home but on the road or in the air, Mike and Rachel were best friends and intrigued by every new sight, every new food. By the time they were teenagers they had stamps in their passports, something I could barely imagine when I was their age.

During college, Mike studied for a semester in New Zealand. In the three months he'd been away from Vermont, he'd matured from boy to young man. With a genial confidence he became our Kiwi guide as we explored the South Island, the magical land of Hobbits. Two years later, Rachel chose Australia for her semester abroad. Of course we had to visit and noted again upon arrival how travel had matured the traveler. We had adventures ahead in the spectacular land down under.

Three days into our trip we slipped from a catamaran into the turquoise waters of the Great Barrier Reef. We floated above the indigo, scarlet, and iridescent green coral, one floating jewel box after another extending for two thousand kilometers. Shimmering paper-thin butterfly fish, lime-green with black tips, swam in nearby schools, while bold orange-and-white clownfish wove through stalks of sea anemones. Black-striped angelfish glided by and in this otherworldly place, I wondered if the heavens were below rather than above.

Only the jellyfish marred such splendor. I couldn't simply enjoy the spectacular swim; instead I tortured myself by dwelling upon what could go wrong. I worried—worry, something I excel in—that a jellyfish would sting us. I'd read about those aquatic devils and knew they could cause unbelievable pain as well as brain hemorrhages. As I mingled with the gorgeous fish, I tried to focus on them rather than how my brain would pound if flooded with blood.

Beauty won. We snorkeled safely in that shimmering sea for two hours before the catamaran crew signaled us to return to our boat. As we boarded, a young woman lay on a stretcher, awaiting a faster vessel for transport to the local emergency room. She'd been the one stung by a jellyfish and I hoped she'd recover quickly. Once the rescue boat arrived, our catamaran glided toward port.

The late afternoon sun warmed my bare shoulders. I could have lolled on board for hours. No, days. Rachel sat between Mark and me on the deck floor and we bumped comfortably into one another with the sway of the boat. "The underwater pictures should be amazing," she said. "It's a good thing *someone* in this family documents our trips."

"I know," I agreed while applying more sunscreen to my arms and then dotting some on her face. "We need you and Mike to be our photographers so I'm glad you don't mind vacationing with us."

She had already adopted an Aussie saying. "No worries."

How I wanted that for Rachel.

The year before Rachel had called us from her dorm room back in the States at midnight. She was weeping and hard to understand as she tried to speak. Sean, the boyfriend of Rachel's close friend, Sophie, had been killed in a car accident earlier that evening. Rachel became Sophie's rock. She rarely slipped under the weight of Sophie's grief but the toll on Rachel was evident. She seemed too world-weary for twenty. Nearly a year later a carbon monoxide accident occurred in the apartment complex where she and Sophie lived. One student died, two others were critically poisoned. Tragedy wrapped itself around Rachel's college days. She knew worries.

I'd hoped Australia's sunshine and beaches would be a balm for her. However, a frightened call came soon after Rachel moved there and was living in an apartment with three new school friends. "There's been a murder across the street," Rachel said breathlessly. "Blood is everywhere." In my pretend calm voice I asked if the murderer had been apprehended. Not yet, she explained. The police suspected a bad drug deal and didn't consider the neighbors to be in imminent danger.

"Rachel," I said. "Be sure to lock your windows as well as your doors. Do not, do not go out alone after dark. Be honest. Is this neighborhood you're living in a good one?"

"Not really."

"Find a new place tomorrow. If you kids need money let me know."

Within a few days Rachel lucked into a condo sublet in the coastal suburb of Surfers Paradise. The girls had a kitchen with granite countertops and stainless steel appliances. From their tall living room windows they watched giant breakers rolling onto the pristine beach. The best features were less visible: smoke and carbon monoxide detectors and a secure building. We all slept better.

And indeed, Rachel seemed most content with her new life on the Gold Coast. Whenever she said "No worries" I'd imagine her big smile. I'd think, yes, she's past those Vermont winter college days when mortality threatened like black ice.

My post-snorkeling reverie onboard the catamaran felt just fine. Sure, I'd feared those neurologically demonic jellyfish because I knew how a day could go wrong. Being a nurse had taught me that, just as being a doctor had taught Mark. However, we felt blessed because our days had gone well. And our kids were close to each other and to us.

As for Mark and me, those good days had been punctuated at times by his stubborn and righteous Jewish bones pitted against my stubborn and righteous Irish ones. Mark bellowed when angry. Not me. I simmered my anger like a pot of stew but on the few occasions when I boiled over, things went flying. Potatoes. Saucepans. Expletives to make a sailor blush. However, as a pacifist, I never aimed at a person. After twenty-five years of marriage we were finally figuring out what worked for us. Certainly not anger, either expressed or repressed. We argued less. Laughed more. We danced in the kitchen while cooking dinner. And on the catamaran beating shoreward against the wind, the sun and the tequila and the closeness of family felt like bliss. I told myself the tough work of parenting had lessened.

We'd all survived unscathed from our kids' adolescence. Mike's primary goal had been to snowboard. Therefore he worked hard academically, stayed almost as pleasant at home as he did with his friends, and earned every mountain hour he could. Rachel focused on her thriving childcare business. She charged exorbitantly, families appreciated her responsibility, kids gravitated to her warmth, and wadded-up cash on her dresser attested to her success. Not wanting to forfeit this gig due to academic or behavioral issues, she maintained good grades, and other than one loud door-slamming year at thirteen, she, too, had been easy to live with.

There were big tradeoffs, however.

The Board of Health, had they visited, would have condemned both kids' bedrooms. They were too lazy to hang up their wet towels in the shared bathroom, so the room never dried out. Mushrooms sprouted through a crack in the flooring by the tub. Mike annexed the dining room for doing homework but then added the mudroom as a bike and snowboard repair shop. Rachel claimed the large basement playroom, and even the dog commandeered my lovely floral couch. Kids not my own raided the pantry, borrowed my shoes, and cooked in my kitchen. Loud music, much of what we didn't like, rocketed through the house. Two neighboring children slept over so much that I wanted to claim them for taxes.

When the kids were young, it seemed that each day far exceeded twenty-four hours. Time plodded on when they were babies and we were begging them to sleep until dawn, when they were toddlers pitching themselves to the ground and yelling "no," when they were school age learning to balance academics with sports and friends, and finally when they were high schoolers and we were just praying they'd stay alive.

Then, Time, the great prankster, played its trick. The years had passed in a blink. How could Mike have graduated from college; how could Rachel be turning twenty-one and exploring the Great Barrier Reef? Our young-adult children were thriving, something for which we had such gratitude. Now we could relax, drop our guard, no worries. Such contentment on that catamaran. Such fine tequila. Eventually Mark tapped my shoulder, meaning *stay awake, Nancy.*

"Rachel," he said, "Let me take your picture and then I'll take one of your mom before she falls asleep."

Rachel stood, unzipped her wet suit partway, and in her bright pink and orange flowered bikini, reminded me of a butterfly emerging from its chrysalis. Tan, newly muscled from running and weightlifting, she looked stunning. When the Aussie crew passed out cookies, Rachel politely declined. So did Mark. Rachel laughed when I said, "I'll take a few please," but Mark didn't.

"Aren't you concerned about your weight?" he asked.

"Of course not." I sniped back.

Rachel glared at Mark, sat down, and nestled against me.

"Mom," she said softly, "You're perfect just the way you are."

Mark's comment oozed like an oil spill across the sun-splashed deck. My weight was the elephant tromping through our relationship because I'd gained twenty pounds since we'd married. Though quite slender then, I packed away food like a linebacker. For years I'd had my father's praiseworthy metabolism, but smack on my fortieth birthday, my internal set point lowered its standards. My appetite didn't waver. Still, no one saw me as overweight. I didn't feel overweight, but Mark often said I'd *let myself go.*

Fran, my mother-in-law, prided herself on being a "skinny Minnie" and with every visit she'd comment on friends and family who had "*let themselves go.*" Perhaps she thought I was also on the train to perdition, because she'd often inquire about my weight. As did her son. I'd smile at them blandly and say, "I never weigh myself." I should have said, *Why are you saying this crap? What does it really mean? Is there perhaps something wrong with how you view food?*

Sometimes I'd diet; *Why not lose ten pounds?* I'd tell myself, be a size 6 instead of an 8. Make Mark happy. But that appetite I had for both good food and my own happiness conquered all. However, I forgot how much kids hear when they're busy listening to Pearl Jam, a band we and Mike liked, or to Hanson, a group Rachel adored but that sent us screaming for mercy. Amidst the house clutter, the noise, our crazy work schedules, the kids' busy school and sports schedules, the weight controversy vibrated with the steady hum of Mark's discontent. The kids heard this. Busy with the incessant chatter of daily life, I'd pretended to numb myself to language, the language passed from generation to generation, the language about *size* and *food* and *letting yourself go*.

The language used in families is either a solace or a sword. Mark grew up with an ultra-thin mother who prided herself on being svelte. To her, thin marked the epitome of success, and maintaining that look was her career. How many dozens of conversations had he heard as a child about those who'd *let themselves go?* Those conversations had wormed into his thinking and how could they not? Those words were the swords in our marriage. I'd explain this to him, but he'd say that he wasn't trying to be mean, he was trying to help me. All I needed was self-discipline. Will power. I didn't try hard enough. I didn't say no to the cookie. And I knew, saying no to the cookies wouldn't define me. I never guessed that Rachel, who had enjoyed so many fine cookies that we'd baked over the years, would ever say *no thanks*.

One evening during our Australia trip we took Rachel and her roommates out for dinner in Surfers Paradise. Sitting at a long table beneath a string of sparkling lights, we feasted on salmon and lamb, mashed potatoes, salads, and loaves of grilled French bread oozing olive oil and garlic. Partway through dinner, I passed the bread to Rachel. "No thanks, I'm getting stuffed," she said. I knew that she'd lost those freshman fifteen pounds she'd hated. Pounds I hadn't thought she needed to lose. Rachel, who had my great appetite, couldn't be *dieting*.

"Gotta save room for the gelato," she laughed.

My little red flag of worry lowered itself. Rachel wanted dessert! Nothing could be wrong.

The next morning Mark, Rachel, and I had breakfast in her tiny kitchen gleaming with stainless steel and sunlight. They had just returned from their morning run and endorphins had them flying high.

"Rachel," Mark said, "I can't believe what a strong runner you've become. You kept up with me the whole way."

"I know, Dad. Pretty crazy. I love running on the beach." She pulled her ponytail holder off, shook her hair loose, then chugged her orange juice.

"Nancy," Mark said, with unmistakable pride. "She's just like me now. A real runner. We might train together for the Burlington City Marathon."

Father and daughter grinned at each other. Back in middle school, Mark had been Rachel's basketball coach. She didn't share his love of the game, the warm-up drills, or fighting for the ball. And when tired, she preferred to sit it out, let someone else race up and down the court. When cut from the ninth-grade team, Rachel cried for maybe two minutes. "Dad will be so disappointed," she said. *And how about you*, I wondered. With that big laugh of hers she turned to me and said *hell, no*.

Yet beneath her banter, Rachel cared deeply about her father's opinion. Now, years later, she'd become a runner, a runner earning his high praise. Of course they smiled about this.

I didn't see, and wouldn't see for months, how regimented that running would become. Only lightning or ice storms would stop her. She no longer chided Mark for once completing a marathon on a stress fracture. Now she'd have done the same thing.

A few days after dinner under those sparkling lights, Rachel and I went shopping. At noon she suggested we stop for a smoothie. I'd been thinking of fries and fish tacos myself.

"Smoothies are so easy," she said. "They're healthy. And cheap. I know this great little shop. You'll love it."

We walked there and bought thick concoctions filled with strawberries, bananas, yogurt, extra protein powders, and vitamin supplements. Rachel promised they'd be delicious and I wouldn't be hungry for hours, but I had more faith in my fish taco platter. We took our drinks outside and found a table beneath a wide beach umbrella. Rachel and I clinked our tall pink smoothies together.

"Here's to Australia," I said.

"Here's to Australia. You know, Mom, I just love it here. Everything's good. School's going well. And then there's Jake."

Jake, the surf lifeguard whom she'd met at the beach, had been the subject of several phone calls. Already I knew more about their personal life than a mother needed to know.

"Yeah," she murmured. "He's such a sweet guy. And he thinks I'm gorgeous."

"Well he's right. And you've always been." So true, but when Rachel grew head and shoulders above her friends, way above the late-maturing boys, she felt gawky and then left out when the little blonde girls were invited to the proms. "You'll love being tall someday," we told her. She'd say, "Probably, but not right now."

Australia, though, specialized in some mighty fine tall men. And were they drawn to her. Especially Jake.

"Things are really going my way," Rachel said with confidence. "I finally feel like I have a little control in my life."

"Control can be helpful," I said, thinking about how control helps us get out of bed on time, do the things we need to do, and most importantly, take good care of ourselves. Oh, how I rued those words when Rachel came to understand them in a different way. Later, control would be the jellyfish threatening her life. But of course, like the young woman who was stung on our snorkeling adventure, Rachel never saw it coming. Neither did we. I missed the significant fact that Rachel had grown quietly obsessive about her running and eating.

"We're so proud of you," Mark had said the evening before. "We admire your great grades. Your running. Your healthy lifestyle."

Rachel felt strong, assured, and had the admiration of her rugged Aussie boyfriend. But beyond those markers she had once again pleased us, parental opinion being her longtime gold standard.

But while we trusted that all was well, our horn of plenty emptied day by day beneath our sun-blinded eyes.

Chapter Two

Vermont, 2005

Three months later Queensland, Australia, yielded to autumn as Vermont hesitantly approached mud season. "I can't believe I'm leaving," Rachel said over the phone. "I love it here but at the same time, I'm homesick for Vermont. I miss everyone." She cried when she said goodbye to Jake but she thought it would be impossible to keep their relationship going.

Rachel's flight home arrived at midnight on a cool May night. Mike was working in Utah for another month but Mark and I, plus six of her friends, gathered at the airport. The kids had illustrated a "Welcome home!" banner for her and unfurled it as she entered the main terminal. Rachel bounded our way.

Sophie, Rachel's close friend, stood near me. Ever since Rachel had seen her through the interminable months following Sean's death, these two young women now watched over one another. As Rachel got closer, Sophie turned to me.

"I don't like this one bit," she said. "Something's wrong. Rachel's too thin."

Rachel did look a little thinner than when we'd visited her, but I assumed that once she settled in with my good cooking she'd regain a few pounds. "I think she's okay," I said as Rachel lunged into me with a huge hug. I wrapped my arms around her and felt a buttress of ribs beneath her puffy down coat. The jeans, snug in Australia, were looser. So I'd watch what she ate, make sure nothing seemed off.

Over the next weeks, all seemed well. What a word. *Seemed.*

In the morning we'd have eggs scrambled with local Cabot cheese, turkey bacon or lox, large servings of blueberries, often freshly picked, and tall glasses of orange juice. Rachel passed on any toast or English muffins, once a morning staple, and with me eating her share, at least one of us gained weight. Rachel and her longtime friend Lucy worked for a caterer that summer. They often pulled twelve-hour shifts, but the generous owner of the catering company insisted that her staff eat like the guests.

"I'm learning manners," Rachel, the liberal college activist and great-granddaughter of an American Socialist Party member, said late one night. "I served at a Republican Party fundraiser, and I just kept smiling."

"You tattle on every tipsy or flirtatious Republican in sight but you never mention any badly-behaved Democrats," I reminded her.

She laughed as we spread Styrofoam boxes of leftovers on the kitchen counter. Greedily we ate teriyaki chicken skewers, crab cakes, veggies dipped in hummus, and vegetable spring rolls fragrant with fresh basil. Our midnight snack said nothing could be wrong, not with an appetite like that. Granted Rachel looked thin, but not gaunt. Of course she torched calories due to running, but with her emphasis on lean chicken and fish, plus the plates of veggies she ate every day, gaining ten pounds would be tough. Maybe I told myself, not even necessary.

That summer, like our Australian trip, marked an easy time for us. Finally home from his winter retail job in Utah, Mike, now twenty-three, had a six-month Lake Champlain research assignment, a job where he used his hard-earned biology degree instead of taking first tracks at Snowbird. Rachel stayed busy with catering and babysitting. I loved having a full house again. Many nights the kids met their friends downtown, had a few drinks, and listened to bands. During those too-brief summer months our phones rang more and noise filled the rooms. Dishes littered our sink and crumbs dusted the counter. If only I had the magic to keep that summer endless.

On Rachel's nights off she did our grocery shopping and cooking. Mark and I felt like company when we came home where dinner awaited us. Our grocery bill soared. "Do you know how much this organic chicken costs?" I complained one evening.

"Yeah, yeah, yeah," she quipped. "You guys buy that regular chicken that's full of antibiotics and hormones. You should know better. That stuff is so unhealthy."

"Okay. You win that one, but does the asparagus need to be organic? We pay a fortune for it and the bathroom still reeks of asparagus pee afterwards."

Rachel had set our dining room table like one of her catered events. She'd found our one linen tablecloth and filled a crystal vase with flowers. She gave me a quick hug then lit the ivory candles. Her fair complexion glowed in the diffused light and she looked like the poster girl for antioxidants and vitamins. "Don't whine," she said. "All you have to do is come home, sit down, and have dinner served to you. That's not such a bad deal."

She was right. But I felt justified about my complaint that she never ate any of the crisp, warm loaves of French bread she served. As if I'd forgotten an obvious fact, Rachel reminded me kindly that bread bloated her. And I reminded her that she'd grown up bloat-free on bread, pasta, cookies, and cakes. Neither white flour nor whole grain flour had ever made her sick.

Mike heard our conversation as he entered the dining room. He flopped onto one of the antique chairs and rocked it back and forth, per usual Mike Levine. Any moment the most recent glue job would give. "Rachel, you're too thin," he said with his usual candidness. "You need Ben & Jerry's ice cream."

"You know I'm lactose intolerant," she answered patiently.

Before, I'd always assumed that anorexia's presence would be obvious if it were ever to lodge at our table. I'd thought that the one with the illness would be sad, secretive, and perhaps angry. I didn't see the way it really happened. Insidious, and wrapped in a smile, tied with a hug.

Mike doubted the sincerity of his sister's perpetual cheerfulness. "Have you ever heard her answer the phone?" he asked us one night as we fielded a barrage of donation-seeking callers. I knew what he meant. Rachel spoke to those callers in a voice filled with warmth and joy.

"Well, unlike you the rest of you," Rachel shot back, "I don't sit on my ass waiting for someone to finally answer the phone." But even then she smiled. The Happy Girl. Mark and I had failed to note that at some point, her big Anne Hathaway smile wore armor.

At least I had the common sense to worry about Rachel's refusal to eat more carbohydrates. I knew that if she tried my dense twelve-grain toast in the morning and then had a few slices of hot-buttered cinnamon toast in the afternoon, once her favorite childhood snack, she'd gain those few pounds. No problem. I discussed this with her while climbing Mt. Philo, a hike cresting to a panoramic view of Lake Champlain and the Adirondacks on the other side. Hiking here has always been our let-it-all-out place. First, I had to catch up with her on the steep incline as she and Bentley, our golden retriever, powered ahead. Stuck behind them in my slow lane I had time to think.

"I watched you climb," I said when I finally joined them. "You're so strong and fast, but you know, your thighs look a little thinner. I think running has raised your metabolic rate. You need more calories. There's no doubt about it." Did my nurse/mother voice sound informed without being preachy? Or worse, hysterical? Oh the endless ways parents must shape language with their kids who are always, no matter what they say to the opposite, sensitive to every spoken or implied word. Tone is a parental art form. Maybe I hit it right that day.

"Mom, I feel fantastic!" she answered without a trace of defensiveness. "I've never felt better about a sport or even about myself. But you could be right. I probably have Dad's super-fast metabolism. If it makes you happier, I'll add some carbs." Again her generous smile and hug. How I'd miss this girl when she returned to school in a few weeks.

The next day Rachel won a 5K race and a quart of maple syrup. She'd barely broken a sweat as we snapped her picture at the finish line. I arranged that photo by one of Mark as he completed the Vermont City Marathon. I studied their identical long runner's legs, thin and muscled, able to carry them for miles. They were fine. Like father, like daughter.

Chapter Three

Vermont, 2006

In his stunning essay "Sip by Sip" Philip Graham writes, "Our daughter, led by an inner voice of terrible discipline that whispers siren songs of subtraction, has crossed a dangerous invisible line." Mark and I didn't hear that voice as we helped Rachel paint her bedroom on the second floor of a faded-glory Victorian rental, her new home for senior year. Instead, we heard her laughing as we joked about the size of this room. She'd need to tiptoe across the mattress that consumed the floor space to reach what was billed as a closet. Her room had most likely been the original closet.

We carted the garage sale dresser Mark bought during medical school up the narrow, curving stairwell and shoved it into an alcove in the upstairs hallway. Then we brought in the first coffee table we'd owned together. It cost ninety dollars in 1979, what we'd considered a fortune, and over the years we'd played countless games of Monopoly there with the kids. Now in the living room, once a formal parlor, the game played would probably be beer pong. I expected the coffee table to be dinged up by graduation.

Rachel introduced us to her housemates, kids who looked much like her in their flannel shirts and jeans, and everyone seemed excited and happy to be back at school. With gravitas she showed us the fire escapes, the smoke alarms, and the carbon dioxide monitor.

"Wait until you see the kitchen," she said. "It's huge and has everything we need. Tons of pots and pans and utensils. I'll like cooking here."

I imagined her fixing dinners like the ones she'd made for us. There'd be plenty of proteins, vegetables, and fruits but she'd need more calories. "I bought a carton of shakes," I said in what I hoped hit the right tone, not that know-it-all mother one. "When you're really busy they'll make a good lunch or snack." Rachel, just as her dad would, checked the packaging for the ingredients. She didn't flinch at the four hundred calories per shake and thought they'd be great.

No, I didn't hear that inner voice of discipline telling her, *What a joke, a drink with that many calories.* I only heard her loud hip hop music pounding from a nearby speaker.

Every few days we spoke by phone and the bright voice I heard sounded full of possibility. All was going well. She loved her classes. Her housemates were easy to live with. She had good morning runs and of course, she was eating well. No worries.

"Are you drinking those shakes?" I asked one afternoon.

"Oh, hate to say this after you got them for me, but they make me gassy. Really bloated. Even if I take Lactaid. But I'm eating all kinds of healthy food from City Market; you know, that place Mike calls City Mark-Up."

The next day I drove the five miles from our home to her house and dropped off another carton of shakes. This time I'd found lactose-free, gluten-free, high protein ones. Rachel thanked me effusively and made no critical comments as she read the ingredients. Several days later I asked if she'd been drinking these supplements.

"Well, Mom, they taste like chalk. Really, really gross."

"I had one. I liked it."

"You like everything," she said and then changed the subject to her coursework, and to how she was aiming for a 4.0 this semester.

A young woman with leukemia develops pallor, bruises, abnormal blood counts, and often bone pain. One developing anorexia is, for a while, at the very top of her game and that inner voice of terrible discipline sounds like the best coach in town.

On a rainy October evening Rachel called. "I just got hit by a car," she cried. "I'm sitting on the curb. I was walking across the street and a car turned right in front of me. I jumped over the hood but hit my face on something. The driver stopped. He asked if I was okay and when I said yes, he drove away."

I saw that small car, and Rachel, long-legged and lucky as a cat, leaping over the front of it. I saw her huddled on the curb, the rain drumming her face, and now possibly in the way of another careless driver.

"Back away from the curb. Right now! Should I call 911?"

"No. I think I'm okay. I can walk home. It's just a few blocks."

"I'll put Dad on the phone."

Mark spoke with her. We agreed that Rachel sounded alert, oriented, and able to walk. Once home she'd ask her housemate for a ride to the emergency room. We'd meet her there.

We arrived at the hospital soon after Rachel. Seeing her in bed stunned me. The red, bruised area below her cheekbone contrasted sharply with her pale coloring. The emergency room doctor gave us a thorough rundown of his findings. Rachel hadn't lost consciousness; she had a normal neurological exam; her films were negative for fractures. However, her face and jaw had taken a whack. Eating might be difficult for a few days. The doctor said that Rachel had been the second pedestrian hit downtown that day and she'd been the luckier one.

I invited Rachel to come home with us for a few days but with an icepack covering her face, she mumbled that she'd be fine in her apartment; she wasn't that hurt, just shook up.

"I'm a little worried," I told her. "You look like you've lost some weight since you moved back to school."

"I know," she said agreeably. "But there's a reason. It's mice. Turds are all over the kitchen."

During my student days I'd lived in shabbier places than Rachel's. I'd dealt with cockroaches and mice, and after college, I'd lived on a ranch without running water. Nothing had interfered with my cooking or eating.

"So you aren't cooking there?" I asked.

"Are you *kidding?* All the pots and pans are contaminated. But the landlord is sending an exterminator. Once that happens, I'll start cooking."

Preparing for discharge, Rachel pulled a sweatshirt hoodie over her bra. Contours of ribs pressed against her skin. "I really think you're too thin," I said slowly, not wanting to alienate her about the weight loss. "Is there a problem?"

"Mom, if you're hinting that I'm anorexic, you're way off, I could never be like that. I love food too much. And don't think I'm bulimic. Vomiting disgusts me. That's the last thing that I'd ever do."

Rachel read my doubt. "Please don't worry," she said. "I'll gain weight once the kitchen is clean. And I'll buy more food on campus. I've just been so busy with classes and running."

She sounded like Mark when his hospital schedule got crazy. Not me. Even during the most hectic shifts I found a few minutes to eat packets of peanut butter and cheese crackers, good rescue food until I could get to the cafeteria. I didn't worry about Mark's weight or his skipped meals. Though undeniably skinny he remained one of the healthiest people I knew. So it made sense that Rachel looked like him since she'd taken up running. And he didn't think she looked too thin in the emergency room. He focused on the fact that no one had ordered an MRI. After all, she might develop a subdural hemorrhage in a few days and bleed out in her closet-sized bedroom. He hated to be that obnoxious doctor-father so could I please call Rachel's pediatrician in the morning and act like a neurotic mother instead? No problem for me. I reassured Mark that there'd be an MRI scheduled by 9 a.m.

We drove Rachel back to her mouse-infested apartment. The rain blurred our vision and as she walked up the porch stairs, we could barely see her. Mark woke twice that night, each time reminding me that *he* would have ordered an MRI. Fortunately, Rachel's pediatrician did. The scan proved negative but for several days she had trouble eating. "Drink smoothies," I implored. "And please come home."

"Thanks, but I'm fine," she said. "Really."

I knew she didn't want to be a townie who spent more time at home than on campus. And looking back I know this to be true: she didn't want us watching her intake, stating our worry, using the words *possible eating disorder*.

Rachel's face and jaw healed within the week. Mike returned to his seasonal job at Snowbird in Utah. Mark and I stayed busy at work. We saw Rachel frequently throughout that semester. She claimed to be eating *tons of good food*, and she ate well when we were together. Her weight appeared stable.

I'd almost convinced myself that simply running and careful food choices had caused Rachel's weight loss. Perhaps twenty pounds lighter than the year before, this new weight could represent a healthy lifestyle. Needing confirmation of this, I spoke with a pediatric nutritionist I knew from our clinic.

I told Louise that Rachel didn't seem what I'd typically considered anorexic and she definitely wasn't bulimic. But she'd been restricting whole food groups she once loved and now could only eat healthy organic food.

No junk food. Ever. And the gym as well as running had taken on a new discipline.

Louise sat down and described a rather recently defined eating disorder termed "orthorexia." She discussed how many "health-conscious people" select very specific food groups. Some might shun dairy or gluten. Others high fat or sugars. Overexercise could be problematic. For some, though not all, malnutrition could become a risk. So could bone thinning.

"Orthorexics," Louise said, "strongly defend their food choices. They view their lifestyle as far healthier than that of the typical American."

Was I orthorexic? I shopped at health food stores and farmers' markets. I bought local meat. I shied away from processed food because I preferred real food rather than a batch of chemicals cooked up to taste like it. I didn't eat much fried food. Still, I maintained a love affair with potato chips and Ben & Jerry's ice cream. And more than once, actually more often than not, I'd stop on my seven-mile trip from the hospital parking lot to my garage and buy a pizza slice or a hamburger to "hold me off" until dinner. For me, balance mattered greatly—trying to eat in a mindful way but, on occasion, spearing guilt-free into a thick slab of steak grilled outdoors.

Was Mark orthorexic? Sure sounded that way. He could cloud our dinners with dire warnings about cholesterol as we packed away our Chunky Monkey ice cream and Cape Cod chips. He knew anything with dairy or red meat would shorten his lifespan. So could desserts. White rice. Pizza. Mark's approach to health seemed rational to him, though extreme to Mike and me.

Louise considered Mark orthorexic perhaps five minutes into my rendition of his diet. Arching her dark eyebrows, she said that it appeared that Rachel was now like her dad. I should watch her weight carefully.

Rachel claimed to weigh one hundred thirty pounds. I plotted this on the Body Mass Index (BMI) scale, the standard measurement relating weight to height, and this placed her in the slightly underweight range. The word *slightly* is a gentle adverb meaning "to a small degree" or "not considerably." This reassured me. As if I could convince myself that something was right because I so needed it to be.

We saw Rachel at least once a week because she was doing her senior psychology project at a nearby center for children on the autism spectrum. We didn't notice any more weight loss. Rachel thrived at the center; we weren't surprised. Rachel and children had a good history.

At age eleven, Rachel took a babysitting course and became CPR certified. She printed her own business cards and walked through our neighborhood, knocked on doors, and offered her services to mothers needing help. A magnet for kids and responsible enough for even the anxious parents, soon she had plenty of work. This solved some logistical problems, the first being economic. Apparently, her paltry allowance didn't cover her fine taste in electronics, music, and fashion. Imagine this: she didn't have a bedroom TV and as she attended Catholic school, her basic wardrobe consisted of indestructible blue uniforms. Hard work brought payday.

By her seventeenth birthday, Rachel had amassed a huge CD collection, a Calvin Klein wardrobe she generously shared with me, a few Coach and Kate Spade bags, her own television, and a shiny black secondhand Honda Civic. If she wanted something, she worked, saved, and then purchased. Of course we took pride in this.

The babysitting business solved another logistical issue. Academics. Rachel coasted through middle school and high school. She never missed a class or an assignment but concentrated more on her friends and her social life than actual course work. Fortunately, she could whip through some of this in study hall and then do minimal studying at night. Babysitting provided an honorable way of avoiding work she had no desire to do. I'd tease her and say, "You must be saving yourself up for college." I felt comfortable with her flailing academic ethic, but Mark chafed at this. "I expect you to do better," he'd say when reviewing the A's and the C's on her high school report cards. "You're a Jew. You're supposed to excel!"

"I'm doing *fine*," she'd retort.

Academics sparked to life on the first day of college. Good thing Rachel had rested up in high school as suddenly school took precedence. A singular goal drove her. Becoming a doctor. Since middle school she had accompanied Mark on his weekend rounds at the hospital. Wearing a dress to look "professional," she'd chat with his patients who much appreciated her visits. One day she spoke with a dying man, and then, a few rooms away, a woman on police watch because she'd purposefully driven over, and killed, her abusive husband in their driveway. Quite the experiences for a thirteen-year-old who found hospital days far better than Lifetime TV.

But Rachel would never become a doctor. No matter how much tutoring she had in college, she couldn't attain the A's in biology, chemistry, and math that were the passports to medical school. Mark assumed Rachel didn't study hard enough but I disagreed. She couldn't have tried harder. Lucky for Mark, he never needed a Plan B; whereas, I had Plans C and D. To my thinking, Rachel needed an option besides medicine.

During her sophomore year at college, Rachel and I had taken a hike along the rocky Lake Champlain shoreline not far from our house. While fighting to stay upright on the slick footing, we discussed all the ways life kicks you hard, her GPA being one of them. She couldn't have focused on academics any harder.. It seemed that her brain, so facile with language and literature, stopped dead in its neuronal synapses at the thought of math and chemistry. We paused and studied the gunmetal water as if answers might roll in with the whitecaps.

"Do you think I should switch my major to psych?" she asked. "It comes easy for me. I could raise my GPA. And after graduation take some of those postbaccalaureate courses I'd need for medical school."

"That's a smart idea," I said. "You might even discover something that appeals to you more than medicine."

"Will Dad be disappointed if I switch majors?"

"Of course not," I said. "He wants you to be able to succeed. And to feel good about yourself."

"But he says I'd make a great pediatrician. It sucks that I can't do math and chemistry."

I put my arm around her. "There are all kinds of ways you can work with kids. Look how much you like working with children with autism."

She smiled. "I know."

We continued our wet hike and then headed for a nearby coffee shop. In those good days we had big molasses cookies with our coffee. Anorexia never crossed my mind.

Sometimes I wondered if those high school C's, ones casually brushed off by "being too busy with babysitting and sports," had reflected a learning disorder. Had we missed this and not had Rachel properly diagnosed? At other times I'd check myself, recalling that no teacher had ever suggested a possible learning disorder. I'd tell Mark to simmer down. I'd asked if there was a Talmudic law that ruled every Jewish child should attend law or medical school.

Psychology agreed with Rachel and each semester her GPA steadily rose. The success of her senior year project not only built confidence but led to employment. Once she had her degree, she'd begin a summer job as a respite counselor for families in crisis. Afterward she hoped to be selected for an AmeriCorps position. A lover of sun and beaches, she completed her application and picked California as her first choice for location.

Steady rain bore down on graduation day and forced the ceremony to be held indoors. This change in venue allowed me to be closer to the stage for photographs. The University of Vermont honors a tradition whereby faculty parents, decked out in full academic regalia, present their graduating children with diplomas. As a professor of medicine there, Mark had handed Mike his diploma two years earlier. Now he'd have his turn with Rachel, and both were ebullient about it.

The tradition was also a milestone for Mark's father, Joe, whom Mike and Rachel called "Papa Joe." Joe, the youngest son of Russian immigrants, had often quipped, "We barely had a pot to piss in." However, he'd made it to college and after serving in Korea, took the GI Bill to business school. To one day see his son graduate from medical school, and then watch that son hand his children their diplomas was Act III of his American dream.

As I wandered the auditorium in search of the best photographic vantage, I noticed four young Sudanese students wearing black suits and crisp white shirts. I recognized a few who worked the night shift as hospital custodians. Sleep hardly existed for them, but I suspected that an arduous Vermont life felt like a blessing after genocide, starvation, and refugee camps. Well-dressed for the occasion, they took their seats among the privileged white kids (some of whom were wearing tattered T-shirts and shorts beneath their long gowns).

Graduation began. By the time Rachel approached the stage to meet Mark, the family cameras were on turbo drive. I waited for the perfect moment for my perfect angle and caught them in profile. Father and daughter stood reed thin and resplendent, the gold tassels on their mortarboards touching as Mark leaned in to kiss Rachel's cheek.

Three hours later our graduation party began at home. Ever gracious, Rachel moved from group to group of well-wishers, thanking all for coming, and catching up on family and neighborhood news. Many of her campus friends also dropped by on their rounds of the local celebrations and the context appeared lighthearted. But in her sleeveless spring dress, Rachel looked not thin like her dad, but for the first time, thinner. One neighbor who'd known Rachel for years asked about her weight loss. We both looked at Rachel's dinner plate, one filled with baby carrots, celery stalks, turkey slices, and vine-ripened tomatoes. Neither the grilled pita bread with rich artichoke dip nor my mother's famous potato salad, foods Rachel had requested for the party, ended up on her plate.

"I'm concerned," I said. "Last week I told Rachel that I'm setting up some doctors' appointments. She says she's fine, but I feel we need a few professional opinions." My neighbor nodded, and agreed that we needed this.

I glanced again at Rachel's plate and thought about the Sudanese boys, their time in refugee camps, then later in Vermont, and I wondered what they were eating at their graduation party.

In my reading about anorexia that spring, I'd found how many resist diagnosis and treatment. Some are in denial with such intense body dysmorphic issues they can't see their thinness or recognize how abnormal their eating has become. Others are convinced that anorexia is a lifestyle choice rather than an illness. Websites such as Pro Ana defend this and offer a supportive, how-to guide for weight loss. Those supporting this lifestyle aren't all confused fourteen-year-olds yearning for misconstrued ideals of cultural perfection. I knew professional women as adept at their careers as fitting into their size two skinny jeans. And as seemingly content with a restricted diet as their friends with more liberal ones. Those women resented any implications about being *too thin*.

I thought about our communal lunches at the hospital. In our brief thirty minutes but often less lunch break, the women staff members invariably talked about food. It seemed that each of us had recently dieted, were currently on one, or were considering starting one after Christmas, or New Year's, or perhaps before summer. Those eating two slices of pizza washed down with a sixteen-ounce soda looked sheepish as the person across the table talked about her Weight Watchers points while having a salad dressed in vinegar and oil. No diets for the guys at the table who ate with impunity. And for the most part, I did too. Sometimes even my patients left me snacks at my desk. Did Rachel fear that her appetite would become like mine again, that perhaps she'd even resemble a younger version of me, or worse, hear her father say, *You've let yourself go.*

Newly twenty-two, and most independent, I expected Rachel to bristle at my concerns about her weight. She'd claim nothing wrong, look at all the healthy food she ate, and tell me not to worry.

Instead over breakfast one early June morning, she said she'd be happy to talk with a therapist and her pediatrician if it would make her father and me happy. She admitted that she should gain a few pounds, but she didn't think anything was seriously wrong. And now that she'd graduated, she had time to take better care of herself. I'd made her steel cut Irish oatmeal and scrambled eggs with a side of fruit and a handful of almonds. She didn't balk from the generous portions.

I smiled on this pleasant morning, a harbinger of gentle summer days following brutal winter ones, for how could there be serious pathology when she had a breakfast like that and willingly offered to see a therapist? This isn't the avoidance I'd read about. I left for my work, and Rachel for hers. A family in crisis awaited her but the one she left behind that morning never recognized the depth of their own.

Full steam ahead into nurse mode, I spoke with a well-regarded young adult therapist I knew at the hospital. Not accepting new patients, she highly recommended a fine therapist just completing her doctoral work. I made an appointment for Rachel the following week. Notice *I* made it. Even though Rachel worked in social services, and had access to many mental health care professionals, I took the initiative to schedule the appointment. Other than making similar appointments for other patients over the years, and of course watching TV therapy sessions, I lacked any real idea of what therapy might ensue.

I got an earful when I arrived home a few minutes after Rachel had from her first session. Her face burned blotchy red. We made tea, put out cheese and crackers, and sat down at the oak kitchen table.

"I'm not going back to that woman," she said. "Ever! She may know about eating disorders, but she knows nothing about people. Nothing at all!"

Hesitantly, I asked what had happened. I sipped my tea when I needed to chug a beer.

"She was the rudest, most insensitive woman I've ever met. She talked at me and spewed generalizations. And she called me anorexic with a 10 percent chance of dying."

I asked Rachel to back up, start at the beginning, but that was about as successful as expecting a racehorse to return to the starting gate after the race had begun. The complaints ran on. The therapist had suggested that there were problems at home and had offered Rachel Kleenex in case she needed to cry. She'd kept asking questions about the family until Rachel felt we were all under attack. Finally, she'd called Rachel *depressed*.

"Well I told her I had a great family and I'd always been a happy person!"

"Did she at least get a history of how your eating has changed since Australia?"

"Yeah, but it did no good because all she kept talking about was my sadness."

I ate my satisfying fix-all-my-problems cheddar cheese and asked Rachel if she'd consider giving the therapist one more chance as she'd been highly recommended.

"Hell no. I said I wasn't going back and I meant it. But I know you and Dad are worried. I'll see other doctors if you want. I'll even sign a HIPAA release so any information can be shared with you. But you should call the therapist who recommended that woman and say her approach sucked."

I didn't make that call because it was too much like a helicopter mom calling the school principal because your child didn't gel with the teacher. Besides, Rachel agreed to see her former pediatrician, her gynecologist, and a psychiatrist Mark had known since his residency days. After these appointments each doctor called and said the same thing. Rachel didn't appear depressed or obsessive. Each agreed that she still ate well, though selectively, and that "she looked just like her father." However, we should monitor this situation and if weight loss continues, consider treatment.

Dana, the pediatrician, said that she wouldn't give a diagnosis of anorexia yet. She discussed foods that Rachel should bring back into her diet and felt that if Rachel couldn't be successful with this, we'd have more concerns. She also explained that symptoms of eating disorders often first occur around a transition, say the stress of high school, or college, or even leaving college;

some even developed anorexia as an adult. I knew one thing: Rachel's college years were the most stressful ones she'd ever had. Anything could be happening,

I'd known Dana since her residency days. Rarely have I met a pediatrician more thoughtful, quietly passionate about medicine, or as good with parents and children. And though the time had come for Rachel to move on to an adult primary care provider, Dana's impressions were the ones we sought. When she used the word "yet" I recognized its significance. After speaking with her I made deviled eggs, something Rachel once loved, for our late afternoon snack. We sat at the kitchen counter, talked about her day doing respite care, I ate as if starved, but she wasn't all that hungry yet. Besides, she now hated the taste of that gloppy mayo. Getting anxious about her refusal, I ate her deviled eggs right after mine.

"We won't have dinner until eight," I said. "How about drinking a small strawberry shake like Dana suggested?"

Rachel's smile blindsided me. "I'd really like a glass of water, but thanks for offering to make me something else."

At Barnes and Noble I asked a sales associate if she had a book about gaining weight. I wanted recipes for my daughter who should gain ten pounds. The bookseller looked as if I'd come up the escalator from a different solar system. She informed me that she only carried dieting books. That's what most people wanted. Of course, I'd even bought a few myself in some half-assed attempts at diets I'd never follow. But now, my mission had changed. Best to be prepared, so I bought the two available books on eating disorders.

Books reassured me; once they'd been the little I knew of wealth. The summer I turned sixteen, I visited a friend at her old Greek Revival farmhouse. She showed me their library with shelf after shelf filled with hardcover books. I longed to touch them, to memorize their titles, to feel their hard spines. Someday I wanted a library like that and to my teenage self, a library represented a well-lived life.

Back then my "library" included a stash of books and women's magazines my mother stowed under the pink azalea bathroom sink in our trailer. At night I'd simmer in long bubble baths while studying her *Frederick's of*

Hollywood brassiere catalogs. How I wanted my own pair of 38Cs and a drawer of lacy bras to support them. However, I never got past the training bra stage. My time would be better spent growing my vocabulary thanks to the *Reader's Digest* column, "It Pays to Increase Your Word Power."

In my bubble bath reverie I designed my future library, one resembling the library in the Greek Revival farmhouse. Years later the reality became a rather generic colonial finished basement with mismatched bookcases housing my fiction, nonfiction, and poetry collections. One bookcase holds tattered but cherished kid's books and adjacent to that, stained well-used cooking books. Being a decent chef, I needed a shelf dedicated to recovering from all my good food. Here rests the diet collection: *The Atkins Diet, The South Beach Diet, The Zone,* and *How French Women Stay Slim*. However, my commitment to the thin life vacillated. Once hungry, I lost all discipline. On a good day I became hungry every four hours but on a bad one, if the clinic happened to be overbooked and we were understaffed, I hungered by the hour. Chocolate, not diet books, saved me.

I placed my new eating disorder books beneath the dieting ones. Quite the juxtaposition. It's odd what I noticed and what I missed during the summer of Rachel's waning weight. I saw the thin daughter of a thin man, and yet in my library, the one I'd been building since my time soaking away in a pink tub in a single-wide trailer, I'd devoted shelf space to four diet books. I didn't see what Rachel had learned from me, the one she called her role model: Weight is important, as important as William Faulkner, Emily Dickinson, John Steinbeck, and Louise Erdrich. Rachel knew the meaning of books for me. A book on my shelf had a reason.

Excerpt from Rachel's journal written as a reflection in 2008:

> *Senior year began and as expected I flung myself full force into academia and volunteering and spent every moment I was not involved in activities at the library. This was partially due to my obsession with work, but also a result of the eating disorder. I felt I had to be on the go at all times, if not in class then studying, if not studying then at the gym, never missing a day, constantly filling the*

day with the same motions in order to feel some false semblance of control. I continued to pretend to those around me that everything was fine but things were anything but. I was becoming fixated around the eating disorder, losing all flexibility and spontaneity, and lying about how much I was eating and how much I weighed to my concerned family.

Academically I was very successful at this time but other aspects of my life began to suffer. Communications with friends took a hit, as I was so busy with school and the eating disorder that I simply could not fit everything else in. I avoided people if I thought conversations would come up which might challenge my eating disorder. If someone was genuinely concerned about the way I looked, my eating disorder told me they were jealous or just wanted me to be big. I continued pretending things were fine but began realizing that things were getting more and more severe.

As graduation approached, the stress I felt inside about what it was that I would do after that time began to grow and grow to an unbearable degree. I felt like I was not achieving anything since I was not already accepted into a medical school or some other outstanding program. I became even harder on myself, more judgmental, more punitive in an effort to mask and numb myself to reality. I placed an unbearable amount of pressure on myself and realize now that no accomplishment that I could have made would have been enough to please the demands of the eating disorder.

After my graduation program I was filled with emotion, with where to go from here, what to do, how to feel, and overall disbelief that I had actually just graduated from college. I had a lovely party with so many important members of my life present in a beautiful display of support and love for me. There was also a lot of concern: people wanted to know what was going on with me and exactly what I was doing to myself. No one wanted to believe that I had an eating disorder but everyone in my life came to this realization.

I pretended things were fine, when on the inside I was suffering. I was a prisoner to the eating disorder and it was beginning to guide each and every action of the day.

The exercising was out of control and extremely obsessive with each *day beginning carefully structured around these routines. Food was completely planned out well ahead of the time and thought out in order to reduce anxiety or being "forced" into situations in which food would be consumed. I would strategically figure out how to avoid social situations involving food, or find some tactful way to explain to friends how I had just eaten, or how I was to return home for dinner later that evening. This thinking was absolutely obsessive and becoming stronger and more invasive as each day passed. The demands that I placed on my body were harsher and harsher and my dissatisfaction with my body increased all the while.*

It did not matter what I did, how much I exercised, how little I ate, what I weighed. It never mattered as it was not accepted by the eating disorder. I could have run farther, eaten less, weighed less, felt less and so on. I began to feel the pressures and feel more and more trapped. Somehow it served to provide me with the structure and rigidity I felt I needed which made the habits so hard to give up. I could not imagine a day without these rituals and literally could not imagine having to leave the comforts of the eating disorder. This caused me to be dishonest to those who really cared for me in an effort to carry on in the way the eating disorder wanted.

Chapter Four

Vermont, 2006

Our house, built in a grove of hemlock, pine, and birch, is four minutes by car from Lake Champlain, fifteen minutes from the Burlington International Airport, and one hour from the ski lift lines in Stowe. This location makes us a cheap and convenient destination for our houseguests. Some stay just a few nights; however, we have had others, those caught between relationships or leases, who've stayed for a few months.

Olivia, a New Zealand native, met Mike at Snowbird in Utah and came for a week's visit the summer following Rachel's graduation. Mike had bragged about Vermont and Olivia wanted proof that it compared favorably to her beautiful homeland. Mike warned me that Olivia wasn't a girlfriend, so please do not act like a future mother-in-law.

A light traveler, Olivia arrived with a medium-sized backpack, a charming Kiwi accent, and a wide grin. It didn't take her long to settle into our library/guest room/media center. During the day Mike took Olivia on trips throughout Vermont. Some were by car in Mike's aged burgundy Subaru wagon. Others were by road bikes. Some by foot. Fortunately the Green Mountains, the Adirondacks, and the sweeping views across Lake Champlain met the high standards set by New Zealand's North and South Islands. The travelers usually returned home by late afternoon. Olivia didn't sit for long and offered to work off her room and board by making our dinners. I couldn't refuse after long days at the hospital. Rachel appreciated having another girl her age in the kitchen and their sous chef Mike chopped stacks of tomatoes, beans, peppers, onions, and asparagus for the cooks.

Each evening Mark and I came home to a candlelit dining room. Olivia's fragrant dishes, always some original vegetable recipe plus a grilled chicken or fish, delighted Mark's heart-healthy requirements. They certainly satisfied Rachel. As for Mike and I, we'd split a bag of chips before dinner. Seeing

Olivia's portions alongside Rachel's relieved me, for they were both equal. Five foot three on tiptoes, Olivia had a small build but nothing about her bespoke an eating disorder.

During one of our dinners, the kids compared their television viewing histories. "Our house was like yours," Olivia said. "We didn't have a TV on the main level either. And my brother and I had to talk at the dining room table."

"If we wanted to watch TV we'd run downstairs to the basement," Rachel said. "Upstairs we read or hung out in the kitchen."

I had a flashback to the much younger days when Mike and Rachel thought our house was haunted. I didn't, but to be safe, neither kid ever went to the basement alone. Though embroiled in some random argument, they'd interrupt their bickering to go watch a show. Their light voices would float peacefully up the stairs and as an only child, I envied such a bond.

As Olivia spoke about her New Zealand upbringing, it paralleled Mike and Rachel's. Academics, sports, and work had played a large part in their similar childhoods on opposite ends of the planet. Now all three had jobs they enjoyed but certainly didn't plan on keeping for long. Olivia worked in retail. Back home, she'd been a barista in a trendy Kiwi coffee shop. "I loved the work," she said while leaning back in her chair. "I knew what my customers liked. I was fussy about how I made coffee. It had to be just right."

"Do you get any idiots there?" Mike asked.

"A few. But nothing like you meet here in the States."

Mike worked through the winters in a Snowbird bike and ski shop. He'd dealt with the movie star who acted like an ordinary guy and plenty of ordinary guys who acted famous and demanded special treatment. The three of them agreed that yes, too many Americans were entitled. You could wait on some nasty people in this country.

I noted how polite Olivia, Mike, and Rachel were. How not entitled. Although their elbows skimmed the table and they used the f-word more than salt and pepper, their *pleases* and *thanks* were abundant. After dinner they cleared the table and did the dishes so Mark and I "could take it easy."

We all took it easy that night. Olivia and Mike decided to stay home rather than go downtown for music and pricey drinks. Olivia took the deep green leather chair that anchored a living room corner, and we plunked down onto the couch and rocking chairs. Olivia pulled a skein of soft yarn from her backpack and began crocheting a ski hat. The crochet hook in her right hand dipped in and out of the white wool like a snowboarder riding through glades of deep snow. The Levines, not blessed in the domestic crafts department, marveled at her handiwork.

Olivia's twenty-third birthday fell on the next day. Early that morning I placed a card and a vase of pink roses and stargazer lilies on her bedside table. Olivia stayed asleep; that evening we took her to a neighborhood restaurant. We laughed when she ordered filet. We thought she wanted beef, but no, salmon. During dinner she spoke enthusiastically about her upcoming Thailand trip. It amazed me how fearlessly she traveled the world with only a medium-sized backpack for company.

As thank-you gifts for her visit, Olivia left a pound of her favorite Kiwi coffee along with her crocheted ski hat. We were thankful for the hat and for the way she fit into our family. Besides good manners all around, Mark and I appreciated how mature these young adults were. Over our leisurely dinners, they discussed politics and life plans, all the while including us as peers, a new camaraderie based on adulthood. They were past the age of eating vodka-injected watermelon, sharing one or another illegal substance around a campfire, or stargazing until dawn on a Vermont field. Mark and I once again whispered how parenting had eased, as if all the years of hard work had suddenly ended. Though they had taken pride in cooking our dinners that week, we took great pride in them.

A few weeks after Olivia left, I heard a sustained shrieking and hopping up and down in the upstairs study. Regardless of her weight, Rachel sure could shake the foundation of our house. "I got in, I got in," she yelled. "AmeriCorps picked me." Her words flew at me. She'd be leaving in a month. And she had her perfect location. Santa Rosa, California, the heart of Sonoma County.

How Rachel had anguished over her application. Every word, every phrase had been carefully edited, and she'd prepared extensively for her thoughtful and articulate phone interviews. Though she had sterling references she'd worried that she might not be accepted. Mark and I couldn't imagine this. We were ambivalent though. We supported Rachel's independence. We didn't want to be those clingy, hovering parents unable to differentiate themselves from their new college graduates. However, we worried about her health. Would her weight remain stable at a weight lower than what we would like, but still not at a risky place? Or would she continue to lose weight after leaving home?

We'd been strategizing about this as we assumed she'd be hired. We told Rachel that signing a contract would be contingent upon her close follow-up with doctors. And with us. We'd visit frequently and monitor her weight. If she lost any more, she'd begin an outpatient eating disorders program. We hoped that if she had the opportunity to do something she felt passionate about, something she valued professionally, it would motivate her to stay well. Thinking about Rachel living a few thousand miles away terrified us but forbidding her to leave frightened us even more. If we lacked faith in her decision-making what would that tell her?

Rachel readily agreed to our stipulations. She registered our anxiety with vows to "gain a few pounds." We collected recipes and meal plans which she "couldn't wait" to use. Other than being slender, the slender of perhaps a runway model, she glowed with her lustrous hair and flawless complexion. Never did she tire or turn grouchy or pensive. The smiling girl's weight appeared to have stabilized. Our days continued as normal as ever. Such a deceptive word, that word *normal*.

Rachel kept busy with catering but on her days off packed for her upcoming move. She wouldn't need much. AmeriCorps provided a dozen multi-colored T-shirts, and she'd bought new jeans and sneakers. She'd take her computer, cell phone, and iPod. She sold the black Honda purchased years earlier with babysitting money and planned to buy a newer one in California. We'd fly out together and in my four days off from work, we'd find a car, do some hiking, and furnish the rental house she'd be sharing with three other volunteers.

All those plans came to a halt the afternoon Rachel and I came home from shopping and found Mike sprawled across the couch in the family room. His face was flushed and when he saw us, he sat up.

"Olivia died yesterday," he said in a choked voice, one so like my own when I'm devastated.

"Olivia?" I uttered.

"Yeah. Her brother just called me. A car hit her last night. She's gone."

I wanted details, where was she hit, how did it happen, what could we do.

But Mike couldn't talk. Or perhaps he wouldn't. I hugged him and he felt stiff in my arms.

"I guess her accident is all over the Internet," he said breathlessly. "You can read about it there."

Rachel tried consoling her brother too. We saw his misery but could do little about it. Mike remained frozen. Mute. He hadn't learned such restraint from his garrulous Jewish father but from his Irish mother. I understood Mike as I did myself. He'd spend the remainder of the day reading a book, though later, probably not recalling much about it. And I'd spend time online reading the New Zealand news and the account of Olivia's senseless death.

Olivia had finished her shift at the coffee shop the night before and was walking home. As she crossed a wide intersection, two cars sped through the red light and hit her. Observers said that the drivers of the cars were boy racers, the name given to New Zealand drag racers. She never had a chance.

I saw Olivia everywhere. Stirring a veggie dish on the stove. Comparing childhoods in the dining room. Sleeping soundly as I delivered flowers on the morning of her birthday. Curled into the green leather chair as she crafted a hat the color of fresh snow. I left that hat on a peg by our mudroom door and whenever I saw it, something hollowed within me as I recalled such fleet fingers dipping in and out of the soft white wool.

"I worry about us," Rachel confided as we packed boxes to send ahead to Santa Rosa. "I want you to call everyday so I know that you, Dad, and Mike are okay."

Rachel had long ago shed any notion of the young being magically immortal. Both she and Mike had heard conversations about death from their doctor dad and nurse mother. In an effort to be open about our work and our own lives, in hopes that the kids would be the same with us, we most likely terrified them. Of course we tried to approach loss in an appropriate and compassionate way, but had we overdone it? Should Rachel have rounded with Mark and visited his old, terminally ill patients? Perhaps it was too much for her when she stood outside the plate glass windows of the Neonatal Intensive Care Unit where I worked and watched the drama of two-pound babies on ventilators with more focus than her friends did while watching the Backstreet Boys on TV. And when Mike was a new driver he hated how I'd just happen to leave the newspaper open with the latest car accident fatality by his morning cereal bowl.

And then the traumas, the losses that pulled like riptides. Sean, Sophie's boyfriend, killed after sledding with them on a beautiful sunny afternoon. The students from the apartment complex who were injured and killed due to a carbon monoxide leak. The murdered woman across the street in Australia, and now Olivia, one month into her twenty-third birthday, plowed down by thrill seekers.

We'd talk about these deaths and Rachel said she could deal with them. She didn't need to work with a grief counselor. She'd prefer talking to us. However, she'd cling to me and say how much she worried about all of us.

If the phone rang late at night we'd hear her alarmed call. *Is everything all right? Is everything all right?* It's not right when a child fears a late-night call just as much as a parent does.

Rachel's eating disorder voice, a voice only she heard, was taking charge: *Good job. Keep doing exactly what you're doing if you want any control in this crazy world. You don't need more food. And you certainly don't need some therapist telling you what to do. You're close to perfect now. And no one will nag you about eating when you're living in California.*

Chapter Five

Vermont, 2006

Research indicates that at least half of those suffering anorexia have a co-occurring anxiety disorder.[2] As Rachel's collage of genes tumbled down her double helix, she had all kinds of opportunities to pick up DNA loaded with anxiety. Worry. Foreboding. That gripping fear tightening your chest and signaling that the sky is falling. It's as if her freshly conceived zygote screamed "more please," and in both Mark's family and mine, we had anxiety to spare.

"I think you need to stay with me so I can have normal children," Mark said the year before we married.

"What?" I asked, because who says something like that?

"Well, you know I can be a little anxious at times. Anxiety runs in my family. It's a Jewish thing." He undoubtedly interpreted my smile as one belonging to a calm soul, one nourished by meditation, chamomile tea, and long mountain hikes.

"You'd be such a sane mother. I think you're the only hope for my future children."

I just about choked on the rich chicken parmesan he'd made for our dinner. My anxious mother worried that her twenty-nine-year-old daughter dated too many men who were wrong for her, traveled too far from her area code, and rode horses itching to buck; and though she had an excellent job, she had yet to own a real bed, save money, or plan for retirement. My mother considered a serious medical student the hope for her only child. Now I was his?

I smiled and told Mark that yes, he was right. I loved him and I loved kids and in the certitude of one knowing little about the rigors of marriage and parenthood, I guaranteed that all would work out.

On our wedding day we combined generations of anxiety. Mark's mother,

Fran, worried that her friends, those who attended posh Jewish weddings in Long Island, New Jersey, and Boston, would scoff at her son's reception at the Best Western Inn in rural upstate New York. I had the bridal jitters for sure when the band got drunk before finishing the first set. Bad sober, they were worse inebriated. This topped only the superficial worry layer, the one easier to joke about.

Fran also worried about weather, money, undiagnosed cancer, Israel, what the neighbors might think or worse, say. She worried about dirt on the floor or a cough that could be fatal. No end in sight for her worries and years later, I'd understand why.

Fran's father fled Russia in the early twentieth century, leaving behind pogroms, a wife, and eight children. Perhaps he'd promised to send them money and bring them to America, but instead, he granted himself a "divorce at sea" and arrived at Ellis Island as a single man. Soon he acquired a thin and stylish new wife. Fran, their only child, lived a comfortable middle-class life until her mother developed tuberculosis. The family played cover-up: pretend nothing is wrong; don't let anyone know what's happening. Finally, years into her closeted illness, Fran's mother entered a TB sanatorium, and seventeen-year-old Fran moved in with a cousin's family. Fran worried plenty about a bigamist dad and an ill mother.

Joe, my father-in-law, had his own problems. His parents, also Russian immigrants, "didn't get along," code for their long separations. Family lore mutates with time and the teller. For years I'd heard about the saint Bubbe Dora who had single-handedly raised her three sons over a fish market in Chelsea, Massachusetts. I'd been given her diamond for my engagement ring and I'd often spun it around my finger, thinking how this woman turned hardship and poverty into kindness. Later I learned that our Bubbe Dora, lively, strong-willed, and unable to obtain a divorce from her "difficult husband" had, from time to time, a male boarder. In today's lexicon, a "friend with benefits." How I cherish this plucky woman.

As a boy growing up in a blighted immigrant neighborhood, Joe worried about the Irish gangs ready to beat up a "skinny kike" on the way to school. On hot summer days Joe worried about the North Shore beach that bore a sign reading "No dogs. No Jews. No Niggers." A generation later he admired how his Harvard Law School nephew purchased a mansion near that same beach. The first time I stood on that beach I spit where the sign might have been.

My in-laws had contemporary worries as well. Too many Jewish boys were marrying Christian girls. A culture that had survived the Holocaust, pogroms, and hate signs was incrementally being diluted as the intermarriage rate in 1979 hit 50 percent. The drunken band at my wedding only spread sticky icing atop the goy wedding cake.

Now add to this my parents who drew anxiety like lightning rods pull fire from the sky. Take my father's job: an electrician for the New York State Electric and Gas company and always on call for middle-of-the-night downed power lines. On those stormy nights he'd tiptoe into my room and kiss my cheek in case he didn't return. My mother worried that he wouldn't and she'd be widowed, she who so depended on this man for all matters dealing with cars, budgets, laughter, and later, just the nerve to leave the house. She worried about her alcoholic brother serving time at the Attica Correctional Facility, the site of an infamous prison uprising due to terrible conditions in 1971. She worried that her only child would turn to the bottle, perhaps not like her brother, but more like her devout aunt, one hand reaching for her wooden rosary, the other for the silver flask stuffed into her bra. She worried that I might not find a good man, a somewhat justified concern considering a few I'd brought home.

"I don't want you going through life alone," my mother said when I passed twenty-five and though I enjoyed being single, she didn't think it a hot idea. Now as my two children had passed that age and were writing their own scripts on young adulthood, I worried in private that they too might be alone.

I was an anxious kid but few knew because I didn't talk about it. I worried that my father would be fried on the job, that my mother would run through her medications before they were due to be filled, that I might make a mistake with my schoolwork, or later at work as a nurse. I worried during my pregnancies that my babies would die in utero or be born with congenital anomalies. And if they were born healthy, they'd become Cain and Abel, drive fast and fatal cars, abuse drugs or alcohol and wind up in either Attica or a graveyard. None of this happened to my children. And Mark called me the relaxed one.

He certainly wasn't. A few hours after Mike's circumcision in the newborn nursery, Mark ran into the nursery begging the nurse in charge to change Mike's diaper and check for bleeding. She wouldn't; she informed Mark to wash his hands and put on a yellow gown or get out of her nursery. And she advised him to never, ever wake a baby.

Mark tortured himself thinking of the possibility of SIDS and it's amazing he never did wake that baby as he checked on him hourly every evening. We made it through that fear but at age three, Mike thought his shoulder blades doubled as wings so he flew from the top of Rachel's crib to his bed twelve feet away. Upon crashing to the floor, he lay motionless, turned blue, and seized. Mark suspected that Mike had fractured his skull or neck and was hesitant to touch him. "Nancy," he screamed, "do something!"

By the time I came running from the basement laundry area, Mike had moved a bit and when I rubbed his shoulder, he began to breathe and pink up. He needed immediate dental work that afternoon and by nightfall, we needed good drinks. The aborted flight left Mike wary of dentists and fed Mark's burgeoning parental anxiety.

Not that Rachel's delivery helped any. During my "easy" labor we watched the 1984 Celtics vs. LA Lakers final playoff game from my hospital room. Toward halftime, Miss Rachel kicked and kicked but never dropped down. As I dilated further and further, she still didn't descend but the cord did and prolapsed. As a neonatal intensive care nurse, I knew the catastrophic emergency this to be. I watched her heart rate on the fetal monitor plummet to forty-five beats per minute. Thanks to an outstanding obstetrician who could move fast and think quickly, we held a daughter seven minutes later. Despite a profoundly low heart rate for those seven minutes, our baby fared better than her terrified dad.

Scarred from this, Mark couldn't sleep unless we kept Rachel's cradle by his side of the bed. It annoyed him that the pediatrician didn't think she needed a home monitor, and it astounded him when I agreed. Therefore, Mark made himself the monitor and slept with his hand over Rachel's chest. Fortunately, she slept soundly beneath that caring hand and every morning, I switched her to the crib in the room she shared with Mike.

After Mike's ill-attempted flight, we had a good year until the afternoon he planted at the end of a slide. This time his teeth fared well but he'd fractured his arm. Mark couldn't watch the fracture being set in the emergency room so he paced the hallway outside the orthopedic area. I cried as I held Mike, but already tough and stoic, he didn't. Naturally, accidents occur at the wrong time. We were hosting part of a progressive dinner at our house that evening and were expecting fifty guests. So I called a friend and suggested all fifty could come to her house—or she could step in for me at mine. Thank goodness the food had already been prepared. When we arrived home, Mike thanked everyone for coming to see his new cast.

Mark couldn't sleep that night. He said both kids could stop breathing at any second, and that's the fear we parents hold deep within us. If it's not SIDs, it's an accident. If not an accident, it's an illness. Once we were lighthearted, but now small lives weighed us down with our worry-tinged love.

However, one overwrought parent is all any child can cope with. Therefore, I exuded the pretense of the calm and assured mother who took fractures, strep throat, viral meningitis, and frequent bouts of croup in her confident stride. I prayed rosaries at home and lit candles at church in case faith really did work. Yet, beneath that confident exterior my worry equaled Mark's and that of all our parents before us.

When does the normal concern about icy roads and downed power lines turn into crippling anxiety? Perhaps when daily life is so impacted that functioning at home, at work, or socially is impaired; when our sleep, diet, and sense of self is constantly under attack. I wonder how any sane person, one fully aware and engaged with others and with nature, can watch the news, follow social media, and not be plagued by an anxiety disorder. Somehow we must cope with worry as a warning that a storm is coming, take cover but not interpret every cloud as the sky is falling.

Quite the task.

Rachel had good reasons to worry. She'd seen peers die young. She craved academic success. She felt Amazonian and "too big." She worried about accomplishing enough good on this planet, as if she were the love child of Mother Teresa and Wonder Woman. Add to all this, she came from a long line of worriers, as if her DNA had been stamped "anxious for life."

So many ways to dampen anxiety. Drugs and alcohol try to convince but Rachel's college girl experiments with Jack Daniels and marijuana weren't a natural fit. The first run on a golden Australian beach was. Better yet, it was legal, inexpensive, and she felt *great*. She'd been missing those endorphins produced from playing high school sports and the new ones coming from a run felt even better.

Soon she coupled this with carbohydrate reduction. Anyone with good eyesight knows that reducing carbs is the one-way ticket to Nirvana. It's promised on magazine covers in the supermarket aisle or in the magazine rack at your doctor's office. It's on TV. Blinking on hundreds of Internet ads. Carbohydrate reduction is fine for those with obesity, metabolic syndrome, or diabetes. Not so fine for a normal-weight runner.

Like the false prophets, drugs and alcohol, running and carbohydrate reduction promised feeling better, being thinner, and becoming your best self. With a new sense of strength and empowerment, and fully enjoying the admiration of men near and far, Rachel noticed something. This lifestyle also quelled her worry.

Dr. Walter Kaye, a leading international researcher in eating disorders as well as the former director of the Eating Disorder Treatment and Research Program at the University of California at San Diego writes that for those with anorexia, dietary restraint and reduced caloric intake seems to reduce anxiety, whereas food consumption stimulates dysphoric mood.[3] Rachel bespeaks his research.

For her, eating less now was soothing, something difficult for me to understand because eating more soothed me. Eating less became Rachel's winning emotional lottery ticket and she was well on her way to spending its abhorrent and dangerous dark prize.

Chapter Six

California, 2006

Joy, Rachel's future roommate, had an aunt in real estate with a most fortunate Santa Rosa connection. After a flurry of phone calls and emails, the girls and two other AmeriCorps volunteers signed a lease on a new four-bedroom house. Rachel shrieked with excitement when our cab dropped us off in the driveway. Some might have called the house just another cookie-cutter two-story suburban house in a development repeated thousands of times across California, but we saw safety there. Baskets of bougainvillea hung on porches, newly planted trees offered shade along the winding streets, and kids played on the narrow green lawns.

As the last roommate to arrive, Rachel pulled the smallest room. Joy apologized and hoped Rachel didn't mind the size.

"Are you kidding?" Rachel said. "My last room was even smaller. Besides, I don't have much stuff."

These two immediately took to one another and an extraordinary relationship began. But that day my eyes were more focused on the kitchen. This particular one had a home magazine gloss with pristine black speckled granite counters, cabinet upon cabinet, and smudge-free stainless steel appliances. Hard to imagine mice running across the beige tiled floor to a homey little nest in the tall pantry. Rachel could cook in this kitchen.

After shopping at a nearby Whole Foods, Rachel and I filled those clean cabinets with the staples of my kitchen: flour, chili, cinnamon, curry, garlic, sugar, sea salt, pepper, rice, and oatmeal. We filled her section of the freezer with Ben & Jerry's frozen yogurt and frozen enchiladas, burritos, chicken dinners, dinners easy to microwave, several pounds of chicken and bags of organic berries. Into the refrigerator went tofu, cheddar cheese, turkey bacon, yogurts, and a variety of veggies.

"I'll eat so well," Rachel promised as we put away the last bag of groceries.

She exuded a joyful positivity, and I fell under her spell. Next, we left to buy a car.

Rachel had been a car freak since her early days crawling after Mike with a plastic dump truck in her hands. She collected little cars just as she did baby dolls. As luck would have it, she'd later babysit for a couple working in the family car dealership. For years, Rachel drove their children around in a series of Hondas, and once, to her real pleasure, a Mercedes. She spoke car lingo. Purchasing her second used Honda came easy as I sat back while she negotiated a tough price line. Quick calls to her Vermont Honda family reassured us that the California salesman hadn't hoodwinked us.

Back at the house we organized her ten-foot square room. It would be years before she could afford a bed frame, but the rug looked like a fine place for the new mattress we'd splurged on. The on-sale Target bedding made the mattress inviting, a healthy swish of Lysol took care of the lamp we found at Goodwill, and a packing box covered with her beach towel from Australia created a night table. As for art, Rachel filled the walls with family and friend photographs, several pictures of our dog Bentley, and a beautiful Lake Champlain scene. Once we had the room all set, Rachel placed her eight-inch stuffed lion on the pillow. We laughed. This little lion traveled to sleep-over camp when she turned twelve, then to college, Australia, and now California. She still slept with her thumb and forefinger clasping its thinned-out neck.

The next day we drove through the gorgeous Sonoma Valley. The mountains folded upon themselves in shades of green deepening to purple as the sun slanted lower and lower. The ageless vineyards looked biblical. We pulled off a dusty side road to a small ivy-covered restaurant.

Oh how we ate and ate. Crispy calamari. Mussels steamed in wine and garlic, angel hair pasta, shrimp scampi, and yes, Rachel even ate bread. We shared a dessert. I looked at Rachel and thought, She could use fifteen pounds. So could her dad. But look at her eat. Yes, she's careful about food and exercise. But truly, not extreme or she wouldn't be eating this well.

"I'm starved when I get home from work," Rachel said on my first call back in Vermont. "You have nothing to worry about. I love cooking in our kitchen. I'm making chicken tonight and a big salad. And I'll have a bowl of frozen yogurt for dessert."

Okay, I told myself. This is all good.

A few days later Rachel found her AmeriCorps orientation regarding gangs inadequate. At the end of each school day, a volunteer was expected to ride the school bus to ensure that each student made it home safely. Rachel said all the volunteers, not just her, needed more information before doing this. She wanted the history of the local gangs. She wanted to know what gangs controlled what neighborhoods and how Santa Rosa was combating gang warfare. Within days the administration offered a more complete in-service, one that satisfied her polite demands. Bubbe Dora, labor organizer and Rachel's great-grandmother, had blood flowing through this girl. We'd seen that before.

Mark and I weren't surprised when pure willpower disguised with freckles and a megawatt smile challenged a used car salesman or school administrator. Rachel rose easily to her sense of righteousness. I'd first seen the public version of this at age seven. Living in Pennsylvania at the time, our property abutted an old vacant farm reputed to be a Native American burial ground. Developers moved in and no one chose to be part of that conversation. However, I'd always asked the kids to be respectful on that land. And so Rachel, leggy and grasshopper fast, jumped directly in front of a bulldozer one summer day as we were hiking across the fields with our dogs.

"Get away, little girl!" the stunned driver shouted.

"Rachel!" I yelled. "Move!"

"You have no right to be here," she screamed at the man. "This is a burial ground and I won't let you dig it up!"

The man glared at us. Maybe it was time for his lunch break because he stopped the engine, got off the dozer, and walked toward the construction trailer. Rachel backed away and we went home. A few days later I offered a story to keep her from halting more bulldozers. I said that I'd called the construction company and learned that no house would be built on sacred ground. Only nearby. This lie seemed no worse than the ones I'd told her about the Tooth Fairy, the Easter Bunny, and Cinderella. However, this didn't curb her enthusiasm for a cause.

In the fourth grade Rachel challenged the school bully on the playground. Ben had been bullying girls and sometimes, kicking them. The teachers were aware but so far, Ben ruled recess. At the end of one school day, Rachel slid into the front seat looking sheepish. She said she'd fixed a problem but had maybe done something wrong as well.

"Oh?" I asked. I'd worked the night shift, hadn't slept well, and had no interest whatsoever in wrong deeds.

"I took Ben behind the school and ordered him to be nice. He laughed. Said he'd do what he wanted. So did I! I squeezed his upper leg like hell. And I told him if he ever bothered me or my friends again, I'd do that to his middle leg."

"And?" I asked seriously, though my inner self laughed as I imagined her doing this.

"Well, he said he wouldn't bother us again. But still, he called me Rat-Chel. I hate that. He says my hair is a rat's nest."

"Hmm."

I suggested not telling her teacher as this manhandling might have landed her in the principal's office and I was way too tired to deal with that. I guessed her action would be effective though. But if this problem recurred, I said, please tell a teacher before mauling a boy. As for her hair, all of us, Mark, Mike, and I, had mentioned that from time to time she should comb those wild, thick curls.

In private, Mark and I admired this spitfire who took on bulldozers and bullies. We never foresaw how such powerful willpower might backfire. Recall that painfully wrought line by the essayist Philip Graham, "Our daughter, led by a voice of terrible discipline that whispers siren songs of subtraction, has crossed a dangerous indivisible line."

The voice of terrible discipline, the part of Rachel springing from work ethic, perfectionism, anxiety, and a growing obsessiveness, had been strengthening since its early days on a sunny Australian beach. Rachel could stride into the AmeriCorps office and confidently state what was needed. The voice of terrible discipline did the same to her. I didn't hear it though. Or at the time, know of its existence.

Instead I heard Rachel's lilting voice as she described her improved eating. I didn't catch how quickly she switched the subject to that of her new students. Already, she had a favorite. Luis. A proud and tough first grader, he came each day with his lunch and all his belongings in the same plastic bag. Everyone else had a backpack. Rachel feared that the kids would laugh at Luis. She checked out the gang colors of his neighborhood—no use in him getting pushed around because he wore the wrong color backpack—and bought him the right one.

"Isn't this amazing," she told him a few days later, "There's a leftover box of stuff in the closet. We need to get rid of some things." Luis peered inside and with a big smile, grabbed his new and appropriate backpack. I had my own big smile as she related this because she'd found work that mattered to her.

We didn't fly out in October as we'd originally planned because Rachel sounded so healthy. Her weight, she promised, hadn't dropped in the least. She and her housemates loved the house. She'd also found some local cafés, restaurants, and a taqueria spicy enough for me. Mark and I thought her in a holding pattern, no gained weight but no weight loss either. A good sign. I remembered an old picture of Mark that I had snapped on a hot July night during his internship year. In that photo he sat shirtless on our patio as he grilled steaks over a tiny hibachi. Every rib popped out as he leaned forward to turn the meat. He wasn't ill or anorexic then. Just working nonstop. Eating irregularly. And so I relaxed during those autumn weeks when Rachel lived in Santa Rosa. Though we missed having Mike and Rachel at home, we recognized how important their independence was to them. They were making their way. Soon it would be Thanksgiving and we'd be together.

In the past we'd had big family celebrations at home in our dining room. Not that year. Mike, now in grad school in Bellingham, Washington, had been invited to a friend's house for their big family shindig. Rachel didn't have enough time off to come home so we'd celebrate in California. We'd hike, tour the wineries, and of course, observe her eating.

Rachel picked us up at the San Francisco airport and we noticed right away that her weight had remained stable. Such relief. "You look wonderful," we told her. She scooped up our suitcases, put them in the back of her CRV, and we took off. Mark appreciated the car for its headroom and leg space, but Rachel's deft driving through the city and on the freeway impressed him even more. Rachel chatted about her work. AmeriCorps seemed a great fit. And the volunteers had formed a tight group. As always, she spoke passionately about working with children. She grinned. Due to a special conspiracy, Luis won the turkey at the annual school Thanksgiving raffle. He couldn't wait to have a real turkey this year.

On the way up the coast we stopped at a restaurant and had large salads and steamed mussels. We ate quickly, dipping slice after slice of crisp baguette into the garlic and lemon-laced sauce. Rachel ate with gusto, once again eating bread, something I took as a positive.

"You look beautiful," I said. "California agrees with you. But you're still too thin to me. I'd love to see you gain a few pounds."

"Thanks, Mom. I know I could use some weight." No anger. No denial. Not even a defensive shrug. "But I'm working on it. It's just my crazy metabolism. I'm like Dad. And probably like you were at my age."

No, at her age I'd have eaten even more bread plus something chocolate and gooey for dessert.

Once in Santa Rosa, we roasted the obligatory turkey and made the traditional, family-honored side dishes: mashed potatoes, cornbread stuffing, green bean casserole, and glazed sweet potatoes. We finally ate at 8 p.m. California time, but eleven for the East Coast contingency. Fortunately my caffeine buzz kept me awake. As did the chilling interior of Rachel's cabinets.

I saw almost every can, every box, every spice in the same exact place as they were on that sunny day we loaded her groceries into her perfect spotless kitchen. Even the frozen food looked mostly unchanged. I felt sucker punched, a visceral pain that screamed how much trouble we were in. "Rachel," I said. "What the hell is going on? You've barely touched this food!"

She smiled apologetically. "I know, Mom. I've been lazy about cooking, so I've been picking up most of my dinners at Whole Foods. After working ten-hour days I'm too wiped out to make something here. But I have tons of yogurt and oatmeal for breakfast."

Perhaps my face looked unconvinced.

"No offense to our roommate, Devin, but he grosses Joy and I out with his bean dinners. Every freaking night he cooks beans. We can't stand the mess or the smell so we just buy stuff on the way home."

Okay, I saw black residues circling the once shiny stove burners that now looked even grungier than mine before marrying the tidiest man I ever dated. Were beans the new mice in Rachel's kitchen? It made sense. The sucker punch pain abated.

The art of illusion is a skill the magician hones to convince the audience of his magic. It rarely deceived me for I was too pragmatic, too doubting. But I fell for Rachel's illusion; some need to believe in magic, I needed to believe we were all right, especially at Thanksgiving.

Thanksgiving ranks as our favorite holiday. We cherish the commotion of family and friends milling in and out of the kitchen, the aroma of roasting turkey, even the routine blast of the smoke alarm as grease splatters in the stove. No matter how hectic the day gets, everything stops for the full eighteen minutes and thirty-four seconds of *Alice's Restaurant*. We sing and sometimes, a dog whines in complaint. We crowd around the dining room table where the political pendulum swings a good one hundred eighty degrees. But on this holiday, we attempt civility, though sometimes a stiff drink helps the cause. After dinner the menfolk clear the table and do the dishes. Ladies take to the living room couches where we often nap through our turkey comas, and sometimes have been heard to belch and fart. That's the Vermont tradition.

In Santa Rosa we had a small round table pulled close to the gas fireplace. Laminated turkey placemats made by the first graders shone in the candlelight and the assortment of thrift shop china and silverware looked boho chic. Mark and I had two platefuls of dinner; Rachel had one, and we all scooped up pumpkin pie and vanilla ice cream.

There's a point in our Thanksgiving dinners when, despite best efforts, despite the stiff drink or perhaps due to it, someone says something that triggers another guest. Same thing happened in Santa Rosa when we asked Rachel about her running.

"Running is tricky here," she said. "You go from a safe neighborhood to one not so safe in a block. It's hard to get a run in so I joined a gym."

"Oh?" Mark asked, "How often are you going?"

"Every morning. It's a good way to start the day."

I laid my fork down and asked how long she worked out. She seemed pleased that she was able to get in at least forty-five minutes but if she got there early enough, an hour, and with luck, even longer.

Again, I felt the punch of Rachel's full cabinets. Sure she could eat mussels and bread, a big slab of turkey slathered in gravy, a plate full of side dishes, and pumpkin pie with whipped cream. I imagined her up at dawn and off to the gym. None of her Thanksgiving feast would have clung to those thin limbs.

Mark and I talked in bed that night. Yes, Rachel hadn't gained weight since leaving Vermont but no, she hadn't lost any and we were in a holding pattern; our intermediate zone between can't-sleep worry and realistic concern. We ticked off similar observations: Rachel seemed her usual upbeat affectionate self, and clearly she loved teaching and living beneath the California sun. She restricted certain foods, though not at Thanksgiving, and yes, she exercised too much. But none of this could be as bad as real anorexia. We'd keep encouraging her to eat better, to consider the counseling she'd been so adamant against.

In those hushed conversations we asked if we'd gone wrong by letting her move far away from home. Yet at twenty-two, Rachel seemed mature and confident about her work, and so settled with her friends. We admired this as well as her financial independence. If only she weighed more.

The next morning Rachel and Mark took a well-planned run to avoid gang-riddled neighborhoods. Instead of using a guest pass at her gym, I made toast and cereal and returned to bed with a book. Later we shared eggs, English muffins, oatmeal, yogurt and berries, and orange juice. Mark's eagle eyes noticed my first breakfast dishes still in the sink. Damn, I should have washed them instead of making a beeline to the bedroom.

"Nancy," he said. "You know how you overeat on vacation. I wish you'd be more careful. You're just sitting around doing nothing instead of working out." Again, I needed that tongue of his bound within an electric fence.

"Mom's fine!" Rachel scolded. "Leave her alone."

And me, flip-flopping as per usual between silence and a wise-assed retort, I opted for silence.

"Nancy," he said as if I needed this lecture, "I'm only looking out for your best interests."

Later that afternoon we hiked the Russian River Valley. Far less dysfunctional outdoors than in, we trod along gently rolling trails crisscrossing the forest floor. Ocean mist, backlit by the fading November sun, framed soaring California redwoods. The spongy earth covered in decomposing foliage and fern softened each footfall. In this vast natural cathedral filled with bird choirs and the pungent incense of tree bark, I offered prayers.

We stopped for photos. Rachel and Mark leaned against a redwood, looking like miniature people with their little stick arms wrapped around each other. In their baggy cargo shorts they looked so alike, these tiny people dwarfed by an ancient tree, that I once again said, okay this isn't so bad. I ignored the gut punch of the still-full cabinets, the diligent time spent at the gym, and instead focused on the father-daughter smiles. Really, Rachel didn't look one whit thinner than her dad. I so believed the sleight of hand, the illusion, that I clicked the picture and we walked on.

Chapter Seven

Vermont, 2006

In 1979 Mark and I forged our ideal premarital agreement addressing the dual housekeeping in our apartment and in our souls. I'd dust, clean the bathrooms, do the majority of cooking, and he'd maintain the floors, shop for groceries, and do the evening dishes. We'd each do our own laundry, a wise idea since I'd turned his tighty-whities pink in one of my loads and later mentioned it during morning rounds at the hospital. We agreed on managing finances without much bloodletting. We'd pool all monies and discuss major purchases ahead of time. As for religion, we'd have an interfaith home. We'd been reading books on this subject and considered ourselves well educated. We wouldn't blend Hanukkah into Christmas and all other holidays would be individually celebrated as well. Every Friday we'd light candles at sunset before sharing a traditional Jewish chicken dinner. On Christmas Eve he'd attend Mass with me, but on Easter, when Jews were taking a hit for the Crucifixion, he'd stay home. Oh, and our future children would easily accept this interfaith model for it would be all they'd ever known. As it turned out, Mark and I knew volumes more about marriage, child rearing, and carrying on religious traditions when we were single than we ever did afterward.

"I won't miss the superficial glitz of the Hallmark Christmas," I promised before our first newly-wedded Christmas together in Vermont. I still hear that ever-so-slight smugness of a simple-life advocate tingeing my voice.

That year proved bleak in simplicity, a quality I'd far overestimated. As a new staff member, I didn't have the time to visit my family in Upstate New York. The nine-foot spruce I'd imagined in our apartment morphed into a cheap four-foot pine with wide gaps between the crooked branches. The tree looked even more pathetic in our living room than it did on the tree lot where it had fellow rejects for company. Mark accepted this stunted little tree as if it were a potted plant but he had no intentions of having a *decorated* one in his house. Instead of the twinkling lights and garlands I'd once loved, I tied six-inch red bows on the sparse branches, thus calling even more attention to their sad plight.

Simplicity left me desiring much more on Christmas Eve. Mark and I were ornery from fatigue. He'd worked thirty-six hours straight. I'd come off the night shift and slept maybe four hours so I'd have time to roast a turkey. I made a mess to accompany it. Gravy congealed on the counter. Mashed potatoes stuck to the kitchen floor. It was unfair, Mark said, that I was such a pig. Yes, he appreciated a good dinner but he was exhausted and couldn't sleep until the kitchen was clean. Never in my life would that keep me awake, so I didn't get his angst. He then called me irresponsible; I said worse.

Here the slide from the ideal to the real skidded straight into pathology. I'd had it with the ugly Christmas tree, a row of night shifts, and wow, the excitement of unwrapping brown ceramic soup bowls. I'd had it with our conflicting work schedules and lack of real time together. And I'd really had it with the audacity of a boy four years my junior, to order me, a thirty-year-old woman, often the charge nurse, to be cleaner, *to get into that kitchen now and make it spotless.*

The Jewish/Christian, Russian/Irish relationship derailed sixty-four days into marriage. No way would I clean that kitchen before going to work. Our small apartment lacked the space to separate Hanukkah from Christmas so I grabbed the menorah, the one from Mark's childhood, and in the tradition of my mercurial mother, let it fly just as Mark walked past the depressing half-assed tree.

"Are you crazy?" Mark yelped. "You could have killed me!"

We both knew that wouldn't happen. Tossing the menorah was the most violent thing I'd ever done. Besides, I had great aim and a strong arm. If I had meant any part of his body harm, it would have happened. But here, on our first Christmas, nothing went as we'd planned when we'd once known so much about marriage.

We talked; I apologized. We kissed within full view of turkey detritus and then I left our warm apartment for the hospital. As I walked through gusts of blowing snow to my car, the 10 p.m. freight train passed Shelburne. I shuddered from the piercingly sad riff filling the darkness.

By midnight though, I felt awake and even peaceful. Perhaps the menorah toss had proved cathartic. So did being in a neonatal unit where each baby was the purest symbol of the holiday and each unspoiled face a morning star.

On our pre-dawn break we nurses sat around the desk drinking Diet Dr. Pepper and eating cheddar cheese and crackers. We swapped Christmas stories and everyone talked about the presents they'd given and received. I didn't say much. How could I compare my soup bowls to their cashmere sweaters, diamond earrings, and skis? But as my colleagues described their loot, I finally accepted my new version of Christmas. The time had come to pitch my old dreams like I did that brass menorah. I thought about that boy, really that man, who diligently cared for his heavy patient load before tending to the picked-over carcass in the kitchen sink.

"We gave each other nice soup bowls," I said. "Don't laugh. We're on a strict budget and besides, we like to make soup together."

Now, thirty-nine years into marriage, we still make soup. The first bowls shattered along the way, like a few of our dreams, but their replacements sustain us through the winter nights.

The freight train still rolls by, its mournful refrain never unheard.

By the time Mike and Rachel came home for Christmas 2006, we'd made some modifications since our first Christmas. We had better trees complete with lights, a few more presents, and best of all, a small crèche surrounded by candles. Hanukkah peacefully coexisted with its neighbor Christmas and my wild bride self had simmered down. As newlyweds we didn't fully understand how the tone of a holiday was not set by the celebrations but by those celebrating them. That education came later.

In 1986 my terminally ill sixty-three-year-old mother vowed not to die of ovarian cancer over Christmas. No one messed with her when she'd promise something. I knew we'd have the holidays together. I bought a beautiful red ceramic church with a snow-covered steeple and set it on the nightstand in her hospital room. I kept a cot by her bedside and throughout those long nights when neither of us slept well, we'd listen to Christmas carols. By then my mother spoke mostly with her eyes. She'd look at me, at the porcelain church lit from within, and I'd think about words like eternity, love and loss, but most of all, peace. I had no peace about her upcoming death. But I had peace about our relationship. We'd had a full lifetime of conversations in our thirty-eight years together and we'd told each other what you'd tell only a best friend. Sometimes during those interminable nights leading to January third, a good time to go my mother said, because it was *after the holidays,* the wind beat against her window as if calling her to a different place. And when that wind did carry her off, her strong voice stayed behind, one no doubt planned for me to *always* hear.

Mike and my mother had a superglue bond as he'd had the fortune to know her before cancer. It seemed fitting to give him the porcelain church. He put this on his dresser with the admonition, "Don't ever turn off the light." The red church glowed for years and how fitting that we rarely needed to replace the bulb.

By the time Rachel came home for the holidays in 2006, you bet I listened hard to my mother's voice. She always said that kids needed love and acceptance the most when their times were the roughest. This generally made me think I wasn't the easy child I'd considered myself to be.

Over Thanksgiving Rachel still looked like she had at graduation. A bit thinner than her dad but still healthy. But as she removed her puffy gray winter parka a month later, she didn't. Her formerly round face had become angular, her chest gave way to a mere swath of freckle-covered bones, her arms had atrophied, and her jeans looked baggier. The visceral thud of those untouched cabinets hit me again. Nothing Rachel could say would convince me that she wasn't anorexic. No more magic shows, no more illusions. We were in those rough times my mother had alluded to. Late that night we sat at the kitchen counter and I hoped to channel her ability to navigate a rough time.

"This is what I'm talking about, Rachel," I said while pointing to the plate of untouched chocolates and cookies. "This is what I'm saying in every phone call. *You aren't eating enough.* Once you would have finished these treats in a few minutes. You're definitely thinner than a month ago. I'm afraid to ask what you weigh."

"Mom, please stop worrying! I lost weight because I'm working so hard. I'm just too busy for lunch. But believe me, I'm not anorexic."

I handed her an angel-shaped sugar cookie. To appease me, she nibbled at the edges. "I'm just not that hungry. I had two crazy flights and I'm beat. I'll eat more in the morning."

"Rachel, your dad and I know you've developed a full-blown eating disorder. We *insist* you start counseling. You can see a therapist while you're home and then arrange for a program in Santa Rosa. Look at you, sweetie. You're gaunt."

Rachel sipped her tea, a flush came into her fair coloring, and she tapped her fingernails against the counter. I knew that tap. My mother did the same thing. It could mean, *I'm frustrated.* Or, *I'm thinking.* Rachel hardly remembered my mother yet she had the same mannerism. I didn't tap my nails because my stubby nails were best kept out of sight.

"Mom," she said, "there is no one who could help me more than you. I promise to begin eating better tomorrow. I know I'm restricting food but I can stop this shit as easily as I started it. If you don't see a change before vacation ends, I'll start counseling."

Flickering candles lit the kitchen and adjoining family room. Our medium-high tree with its modest three strands of white bulbs sparkled by the brick fireplace. And for that perfect Vermont night, snow laced the hemlocks ringing our backyard. Rachel covered my hand with hers.

Mike had inherited my mother's tawny hair and ease with language, Rachel her graceful hands, and as she clasped my own, I felt the palpable presence of three generations.

"Mom," Rachel promised and I think she believed her words, "We can do this. We can make it better. Tomorrow will be different!"

She dazzled me with her smile.

"Christmas magic," she murmured. "You just wait and see."

"Let's hope," I said while staring at the angel atop our tree. "You know how I always say that feeling your first kick during Christmas Eve Mass was a celestial sign that you'd be healthy."

Sitting close, we nudged one another.

"And then there was my birth."

"Yep. Hard to forget that little drama."

"So, Mom, you and I can get through anything. I really will change. I have to admit I'm hungry," she said and proceeded to eat the entire cookie she'd been jockeying around her plate.

In the morning Rachel had no trouble eating a real breakfast: eggs, turkey bacon, two slices of toast, and yogurt topped with berries. She and Mike then went downtown to do their Christmas shopping. Hours later, they returned, shopped out, broke, but genial. They'd met friends for lunch and had a good day. It seemed like the old times before Rachel's food restrictions. She enjoyed a big dinner and even dug into a bowl of Ben & Jerry's ice cream. I felt buoyant by the time we left for Christmas Eve Mass.

Even the music rose to the occasion. In the past our parish had well-meaning but lackluster adult voices. This year the high school kids and their musical director changed all that. One student, a senior headed for an opera career, stunned us with the quality and range of his voice. But then a young soprano, one who had never sung in public, did the same. Regardless of the fact that we were in Mass, and in an often-subdued congregation, we clapped loudly for each gorgeous selection. As we drove home, again in that storybook Vermont snow, we agreed that we felt inspired; though, it being after midnight, we were too tired to say how. Besides, knowing that Rachel would have us up at dawn to open gifts, we just wanted to sleep.

Rachel's appetite was our best gift.

By the end of her weeklong vacation, I knew Rachel's eating issues had resolved. Had it been a Christmas miracle, had those soaring notes during Mass settled into her soul, had my mother sprinkled guardian angel dust upon her?

On her last night home we sat by the waning fire in our family room. "I think I'm better," she said.

"I think so," I answered. "For a while there you had Dad, Mike, and I pretty worried. I'm so happy that it's over. I couldn't have had a better Christmas."

The nurse in me knew how difficult overcoming an eating disorder could be. I'd known patients with years of struggles. Countless attempts at counseling. Countless relapses. Yet the believer in me, the one who skipped Mass for months at a time, said miraculous cures can happen.

Mark didn't ride my miracle train. Ever more rational, he pointed out that Rachel had "come to her senses in the nick of time." He'd seen this before with medical students and residents who'd developed eating disorders during their stressful training years.

Mike simply said, "Keep eating." And if there was one voice Rachel heard the most, it belonged to her brother.

On that last night at home we made menus for Rachel to use in Santa Rosa. She agreed to weigh herself weekly and call me with that number. Now this didn't sound like someone suffering an active eating disorder.

Rachel checked her weight before leaving.

"I gained three pounds," she said.

My joy deafened me to the anxiety in her voice. Anyone with a lick of sense, anyone understanding triggering behaviors, would gasp, maybe choke from my words. "Rachel," I said in unmitigated stupidity, "look how easily you gained weight. Why you'll be back to your normal weight in no time." My blather rolled on. I took her pensive look to be one of quiet joy from the Christmas miracle.

The next morning I drove her to the airport. Wispy snowflakes flew at our headlights and a bitter wind cut through me as we hugged outside the terminal. "Go back and get some rest," Rachel said. She smelled like fresh coffee and Burberry perfume, and it hurt to release her. The snow grew heavier as I drove home in the flat, graying light but I didn't mind the weather. The illusionist, Anorexia Nervosa, had duped me with the best illusion yet, and I smiled.

Rachel's eating disorder voice: *Wait until you get back to Santa Rosa. How could you have been such a slacker? How could you have let yourself go? You ate like a pig. You gained THREE POUNDS in one week. Do you see how easy it was? You'll be fat in no time! By the way, gaining weight is no miracle. It's being out of control. You messed up. You're a failure.*

Chapter Eight

California, 2007

In January I questioned Rachel's health and our almost daily phone calls gave me reasons to. In answer to my direct questions, she said no, she hadn't gained any weight and maybe she'd lost a few pounds. But we shouldn't worry because she *was* trying hard to eat more. I gave her the names of a few eating disorder treatment centers in her area and encouraged her to make an appointment.

"Mom," she said adamantly, "I can turn this around. I'm eating every meal. It's just my metabolism."

"It's always your metabolism."

"Please, Mom. Stop pressuring me! If I thought I had a problem, I promise I'd get help."

The conversation dead-ended.

After her abrupt weight gain at Christmas, Rachel had slipped back into anorexic behaviors that felt as good to her as kicking your shoes off at the end of a long day. Of course we didn't know this. No way did she want us to.

But then it came via another phone call. I knew by the shudder in her voice that something had happened.

"Mom," she sobbed. "Luis came to school today. He's okay but his family—his grandparents, his aunt and uncle, and little cousin—were on the freeway and hit from behind. Their car caught on fire. A bystander broke the back window and one of the relatives pushed the cousin through the back window."

This image alone horrified me.

"Then the car exploded. Everyone else died."

After a protracted silence, then gasps, Rachel wanted to know how, if God really existed, could a family be incinerated? A family who'd left

Mexico for a better life, a safer life. She wanted my answers, but I lacked any intelligible ones.

This is when living a few thousand miles from family is almost impossible. You can't pull a grieving child into an embrace. There's no body language to show *I hear you, I understand you.* You can't make that person a cup of coffee or a bowl of soup. Your words must substitute for all these things and what happens when mere words, stripped of any physical contact or those small acts of grace, are inadequate? How often can you say, *I'm sorry, this is beyond tragic?*

I couldn't sleep that night. I kept seeing a child being lifted from that inferno. And if I didn't sleep, I knew that Rachel didn't either. She remained understandably shaky in the morning. Days passed and she didn't rebound well from this accident. Mark and I recognized her shock, sorrow, and anger at the world but we could only offer long-distance love. I asked her if it might help to meet with a therapist. Her answer came fast. "I tried that once and it was worth shit."

What did seem to help her, and hopefully Luis, was the extra time that they spent together after school. For Luis, she could be a rock, just as she had for Sophie a few years earlier. But now this rock was crumbling, but of course, we couldn't see it. But we'd hear fear when she'd whisper into the phone that she worried about her father, Mike, and me.

"I can't have anything happen to you," she said soon after that accident.

What we couldn't see, and didn't hear about, were the new rituals she'd developed. The voice of terrible discipline instructed her to drive a certain way to school. If she didn't do this, something might befall us as well. She couldn't finish a muffin at the coffee shop because each bite was a misstep representing the childhood chant, *Step on a crack and break your mother's back.*

We should have flown out in January, but we had new distractions. Mark's mother, Fran, had developed pancreatic cancer and at eighty-four, didn't want aggressive treatment. Our first visit after her diagnosis was rife with conflict.

We sat around Fran and Joe's white kitchen table that Joe had laden with turkey, pastrami, roast beef, chopped liver, egg salad, potato salad, tossed salad, wheat bread and rye, two kinds of pickles, Dr. Brown's Cream Soda, orange juice, coffee and all this only a prelude to three kinds of cake and a tray of rainbow cookies.

Joe and I were stressed and eating enough to prove it. This aggravated Fran. "Joe," she said, "Look at your big fat stomach. How can you eat so much?"

I knew exactly how he could.

Then she looked my way and mentioned my huge appetite. Mark followed up with the comment that maybe I'd already had enough for lunch. Fortunately Joe and I were spared more controversy because we moved on to Fran's illness and the recent procedure to place a temporary stent into her blocked pancreatic duct. Husband and son implored her to have surgery, followed by chemo and radiation. I urged Fran to at least discuss her options and then make choices for herself.

Fran looked cornered. "I don't want to talk about this," she said.

"But you have to," Mark shot back. "The stent is only temporary. It could occlude at any time and you'd be sick again. You'd need to be hospitalized immediately and who even knows if another stent would work. Or if it did, how long it would last."

I imagined myself at eighty-four and how I'd feel in Fran's position so I understood when she repeated that she didn't want to talk about treatments.

Mark's not easily swayed. "But you have to. That's why we drove here!"

Fran looked at her older son, cocked her eyebrows the way I'd seen dozens of times, and with an undisputed finality, pushed her hands towards us. "Who needs this?" she said and left the table. Joe followed her to their room and we could hear yelling. We went home the next day without any resolution. We'd return in a few weeks for the same conversations.

Winter had settled in our bones. Black ice threatened us daily.

Rachel planned to visit her grandparents in February. She wanted to check on them; we needed to check on all of them so we agreed to meet the weekend before Valentine's Day.

We arrived in Toms River a few hours after Rachel. Not surprisingly after taking the red-eye to Philly, and then a shuttle to New Jersey, she was napping on the family room couch. I'd last seen her in the dim snowfall at the Burlington airport, that morning of great hope. Five weeks had brought more weight loss; the figure beneath the blanket belonged to a child. The visceral thud of her appearance left me breathless. No one could mistake her skeletal outline.

Fran teetered from her bedroom. Cancer had stripped more weight leaving her nearly as gaunt as Rachel. Joe walked behind, his hand poised to catch her in case she collapsed.

"Hi, kids," he said as if we were one happy and healthy group. "I got such a spread from the deli. You should all sit down. And we'll wake Rachel up. She needs a good meal."

"I'm not hungry," Fran said. "Why do you have to buy this much stuff?"

So we sat at this overfilled table, grandmother cachexic, wasting from cancer, granddaughter anorexic, and one trying to make the other eat. Fran raised her tired eyes to Rachel. "You should have something, darling; you're too thin."

"And you too, Mama Fran. Everything looks delicious. But I ate so much junk on the plane that I'm stuffed." Maybe to please us, or perhaps quiet us, Rachel had a slice of turkey, half a plate of vegetables, some fruit, and her favorite Jersey tri-colored cookies.

As we'd agreed that Fran needed rest, the three of us left after lunch and went to a nearby hotel. Even Joe, who normally liked us all crammed in together in their retirement home, thought this wise. Now we also needed privacy to deal with Rachel.

Our hotel room had a small couch. Rachel and I sat side by side, her shoulder a bony wing pressing into me. Mark sat opposite in a chair designed for tight spaces and short people. His long arms hung over the armrest; his legs stretched across the rug. Nothing about him appeared comfortable.

"Do you know how thin you are?" Mark asked Rachel. "Do you have any idea how much weight you've lost since Christmas? Your mother and I are very, very concerned. This is serious. You could die if this continues. Are you aware of that?"

"I know I need to gain weight," Rachel said, devoid of expression and so unlike her former animated self. "But I feel fine. I'm sorry that you two are worried about me."

"I think you're clueless," Mark said gently. "You have no idea how you look. Are you okay with me taking pictures of you? If you see how you look, maybe you'll start therapy like we've been asking."

Rachel agreed to this. We'd been planning to swim in the hotel pool so she said she could be photographed in her bikini.

How can this be Rachel, I thought as I looked at her. How had this happened to her, of all people? What did we do wrong when we tried to do everything right? Mark finished photographing her, took the film to a one-hour kiosk (necessary in the age before everyone had a cell phone with a camera), and Rachel and I went for our swim.

A vaulted glass ceiling allowed winter sunbeams to fall across the pool. Huge potted plants lined the deck and if I pretended hard enough, we could be somewhere tropical. If I pretended even harder, the girl swimming beside me would be the one from the Great Barrier Reef. But it was February in Jersey and we were fresh out of pretense. However, Rachel and I could still be playful in the water and for too brief a time, we were lighthearted.

Mark had the newly developed photographs waiting for us when we returned to the room.

"The mission of photography," Edward Steichen wrote, "is to explain man to man and each to himself.[4] And that is the most complicated thing on earth." We were about to learn this as we stared at those haunting images.

"Do you see what I see?" Mark asked. Frustration accented his words. "Look at you."

I saw what Mark did. Long skeletal limbs, concave stomach, hip bones jutting over the twin concavities once rounded with muscle and flesh. A stranger's elongated face.

"How do you see yourself?" I asked. My voice trembled.

"I look horrible," she admitted. "I know how bad I look. I can't—I can't believe I've done this to myself. I feel so guilty."

"Honey," I said. "Don't feel guilty. This is an illness and it isn't your fault. You'll get better but you must get help now. There's no alternative."

"Okay," she cried. We held her and she promised to get well.

Some with anorexia never see themselves as thin enough. Due to a body dysmorphic disorder, they see roundness in a shrunken stomach, or thick legs as opposed to thin ones. Rachel saw herself as we did. What we didn't grasp was how powerless she was, how changing the equation from sickness to health was a complex problem with variables depending on neurobiology, neurochemistry, nutrition, and extraordinary counseling.

I'm not sure if those pictures met Steichen's high bar of photography but in this painful time, Rachel's acquiescing to therapy felt steps closer.

Before leaving to meet the grandparents at a nearby seafood restaurant, I called Fran and explained how rough our afternoon had been. "Please," I said, "don't discuss Rachel's weight or how she may be eating. For a few hours we need to back off, give her some downtime, and maybe she'll eat better if she isn't feeling watched."

"Of course, darling," Fran said. "See you soon."

While we were waiting for dinner I sketched a few anatomical drawings of Fran's cancer. Mark and I hoped a visual representation would lend clarity to her condition. We were using our professional identities as shields, as if our photographs and drawings might divert our raw emotions into something quantifiable and understood once rendered in black and white. But the real deal, a phrase Joe loved, came down to this: Fran had a fatal illness, Rachel a possibly fatal one. We felt bogged down with grief, but as usual, couldn't even manage something simple like getting to dinner on time.

The older Levines, always on time, awaited us at the table. We apologized and they said, "No problem. Glad you had a safe trip. The roads are icy tonight. Just awful out there." Fran gave me a long, hard once-over as I removed my winter coat.

"You lost a few," she said, ever the weight police. "You look good."

I glared back. I told Fran not to mention Rachel's weight. I thought it obvious that she shouldn't mention *anyone's*. I hated my glare; couldn't I give this woman a break considering her age and health? I forced a low wattage smile and sat down. Partway through our meal, that weak smile burned out when Fran pointed to Joe's stomach. "Look at how fat he's gotten," she said. "It's not healthy."

"Yeah, yeah, yeah," Joe volleyed back. Her words didn't suppress his appetite in any way. But I worried what they might do to Rachel. She, like her brother, had grown up close to these grandparents. So many wonderful trips to the shore they'd shared. So many vacation weeks where the kids stayed up late, watched movies, and even played shuffleboard with a coterie of retired neighbors and friends who treated all grandkids like their own. What Fran and Joe said and did mattered to Rachel.

I did the pretend-casual look at Rachel. After dicing her food into pea-sized bites and moving them around her plate like chess pieces, she eventually finished most of her scrod, all her green beans, and part of a baked potato.

Again she claimed to be stuffed.

After dinner, Joe and I shared a mighty fine piece of double chocolate cake that no one else wanted. There's nothing like eating on the Jersey Shore but even this sweetness couldn't abate the sadness at the table. While awaiting our bill, I asked Fran how she felt. Not a question she liked, but how could we go through the evening and not ask? She mumbled that she felt okay, but she didn't want to talk about it. Mark remained mute and needed me to be the one cracking open the conversation. I passed my drawings across the table to her.

"I thought you might like a better understanding of where all this trouble is," I explained. "Sometimes it's easier to understand what's wrong if you can picture it."

Fran gave a cursory glance at my five sketches. She brushed her arm downward from her neck to below her waist, a representative showing of all the places she knew to be under attack. "Who needs it?" she said. "How's the weather been in Vermont?"

Mostly I wanted the weather in the sun-filled pool and the way it buffered the tension between Rachel, Anorexia, and me. "February has been miserable," I said. "But please, take these pictures home. Maybe look at them later."

Mark offered to answer any questions and to ask her doctors to call him. Fran liked this. In this uncertain dance we stumbled through, both Fran and Rachel felt free to share all their medical information with us. One of our few advantages. As difficult as knowing could be, not knowing is worse.

On the way back to our hotel we navigated all kinds of ice. Rachel spoke with sadness about her grandmother's appearance.

"You look even thinner," I countered. "Can you understand why Dad and I are terrified?" In the long-upheld tradition of the tallest in the front, the shorter ones in back, I leaned forward from my seat and massaged Rachel's shoulders, something she always appreciated during long car trips. My fingers rubbed bone.

"Your dad and I were thinking about you not returning to Santa Rosa. You'd certainly get a medical leave of absence. I did some checking around and there's an excellent residential program nearby. You could be admitted and we'd visit every weekend. And you'd be close to your grandparents." What magical thinking prompted me to see Rachel willingly dropping everything and sashaying into an eating disorders treatment center?

"I hope you haven't been going behind my back and setting something up!" she countered with a ferocity rarely directed at me. "I *said* I'd begin outpatient therapy so be happy about that. Stop pressuring me. I'm an adult and I know what's best for me. I'm not irresponsible. So there's no way I'd leave my job before my contract ended. I just wish you'd stop talking about this for once!"

We did. She'd be back home in another few weeks and we'd talk about it then.

The next morning we took Rachel to the Newark airport and from there, drove to Vermont. Traffic snarled the interstate. Horns blared, human fuses blew out, and cars zigzagged between lanes at eighty miles an hour, a made-for-disaster ending to our blighted weekend.

Chapter Nine

Vermont, 2007

March in Vermont is merely winter with longer days but for Rachel in Santa Rosa, spring break had arrived along with time to fly home. Though the sky dropped sleet bombs as I drove to the airport to pick her up, I felt almost happy. Rachel had begun therapy at an eating disorders center. With my endless faith in good treatment and her voiced determination to get better, I dared to think she'd gained a few precious pounds.

Rachel bounded across the airport terminal with her long-legged strides and warm smile. As we hugged, her Burberry perfume settled on me. But then, I felt her ribs and I knew, despite treatment, she'd grown bonier. The new size two ivory corduroy jeans once snug in February hung like clothes on a scarecrow. Her eyes appeared cavernous over sunken cheeks. My endless faith needed a reality check.

"So good to see you," Rachel shrieked.

"I'm so glad to see you!"

"You look great, Mom."

"You too," I lied, and thought *you look thinner, paler, sicker*. Why did I think three weeks of therapy could possibly halt this progression?

To all appearances as we walked to the baggage carousel, we were like any mother and daughter happy to reunite. No tension, no darkness between us. Rachel was Vermont chic in her gray down coat, beige Ugg boots, and scuffed up blue backpack cinched high on her shoulders. In jeans, thick boots, and a dog-haired black parka, I looked like a standard Vermont mother.

"How's Dad?" Rachel asked while we waited for her overstuffed suitcase.

"Good. He's coming home early. I made fish stew."

"I love that! Just wish Mike could be here."

So did I. We'd seen Mike at Christmas but since he was busy with grad school in Bellingham, we wouldn't see him until summer. All our weekly phone calls included his concern about his sister. He knew, as we did, that she listened to him more than she did to us. But now she disregarded whatever he said about her eating.

Rachel lacked no strength as she wrestled her jumbo-sized suitcase off the conveyor and tugged it behind her. As we exited the terminal a blast of Canadian air ripped across our faces.

"Now this must feel like home," I quipped.

I gave her my car keys and as we drove home, I asked about her students. All were amazing and read better with each day. They hoped I'd visit their classroom soon and read to them. She wished I'd visit so we could hike in the Russian River Valley and enjoy some wine tastings. We drove home amid easy chatter.

Easy car chatter became tumult as the daily drama of anorexia played out in our kitchen and dining room. The kitchen, once my favorite room, faced our woods and from here we had watched the pin oaks change colors in autumn, drop desiccated leaves, and come spring, surprise us again. Here we'd had thousands of breakfasts. Big buffets. Conversations writ large and small, and now, so much turmoil, spoken or not.

On Rachel's first night home she sat at the counter while I finished the cioppino that she and Mark love. "I'm so hungry," she said. I believed her. Rachel still had hunger signals. Though she'd ignore them, she certainly felt hunger, but later those signals would drop like those desiccated leaves.

We set the dining room table and I lit the ivory candles as if they were votive lights in the side altar at church. I prayed for the night ahead. Cioppino has little fat, sugar, and cholesterol. It's lactose-free, gluten-free, and somehow still manages to taste good. Especially with wine and wedges of bread to scoop up the broth. I filled three large bowls of this winner of a stew for the heart-healthy and thought the low calorie count wouldn't upset Rachel. We sat down, took our places on the dining room stage, and all went wrong.

Rachel looked as if she'd been cinched into a bomb vest. She barely touched the soup with her spoon. Normally chatty, the very presence of food had silenced her. I wanted to shout, *eat something, eat something, how can you live like this?*

"I think," Mark suggested, "that you should take some bread to dip."

She could barely dip her spoon, let alone a chunk of grilled focaccia, into what proved not to be a winner of a stew. Minutes passed. Rachel finished half her cioppino. None of the bread.

"Rachel, this soup is full of protein," I said in tumult. "You must try harder."

"I'm sorry, Mom. This is delicious but I can't eat anything else. My nutritionist has set goals for me. Each week I'll add a slightly larger portion but for now, I'm meeting his goals and mine."

"But Rachee, you ate more when you were a little girl."

"Mom, there you go! You said you wouldn't pressure me."

"Your mother is right, Rachel. Just have a little more." For once Mark didn't sound like a doctor. He sounded like a terrified father.

Although Rachel couldn't eat more, I could and lit into seconds of cioppino, bread, salad, and that lovely merlot before noticing Mark's critical look.

"Nancy," he said tersely, "Just because Rachel can't eat doesn't mean that you should eat twice as much as usual."

"Dad, leave Mom alone!" Rachel blazed back.

If Rachel hadn't been at the table, the aging wild bride would have tossed a potato, but I knew that would only trouble her more. I stayed silent. Rachel looked wounded. So went the drama, center stage in the Levine dining room, the year Rachel disappeared from us. Clearly, lighting candles for our family in church and at home wouldn't be the entire solution.

As a teenager I wrote on a narrow, built-in laminate desk in our trailer. I liked the intimacy of the eight-by-ten-foot space, the lemony smell of the paneling my mother rubbed with Cabinet Magic, the gold sateen spread hugging the wall beneath the transom window. My words carried me to a faraway sea and my room was a cabin on a yacht. Now, so many years later, my writing space isn't much bigger. Mark and I share a small "study" in the Vermont woods, and we share the same desk as well. His drawers are on the left, mine on the right, and tight as the room is, it's been a compatible arrangement. Long ago I succumbed to the chaos of crowded bookcases, reams of paper, printers, at least two laptops, and a big blonde retriever wedged under the desk and over my feet.

Two nights after the bomb vest dinner, I asked Rachel to watch Lauren Greenfield's documentary *Thin* with me in this messy place. We sat at the desk, our shoulders touching, and I explained that I'd already seen this film about four women in an eating disorders treatment center. Now she should see it.

"Just in case your outpatient program isn't enough support," I said, "You might need to consider a residential center."

"I love my therapist and my nutritionist. They're amazing. Wait until you meet them next time you visit. I won't need another program but it's good to see what's out there."

"Definitely. You never know." But I did. She restricted food more than in February. I estimated she was taking in maybe nine hundred calories daily and rarely missed a workout or run. According to her, she met all the goals her therapy team set. She wasn't leading me on. Rachel had given HIPAA permission for their information to be shared with us. Transparent in many ways, we could know her treatment plan, her progress, her lab values, and her vital signs. However, what the scale read stayed private; she was over twenty-one and we could only guess her actual weight. I'd spoken twice with her nutritionist and therapist, and both reported that Rachel was a pleasure to work with and was highly motivated to get well. She'd been responsive to all their suggestions and both expected a solid recovery. They understood my anxiety but said I should have patience and wait for Rachel to have an ah-ha moment, a time when she'd turn this whole illness around.

I felt encouraged after those calls but watching Rachel micromanage every meal made me doubt my optimism. I thought that watching *Thin* together might shock Rachel into her ah-ha moment of self-discovery and action. She needed that fast.

In a gut-wrenching documentary, Greenfield immersed herself in the culture of the Renfrew Center, a forty-bed residential program in Coconut Creek, Florida. The film opened with bold black print on a white background.

Eating disorders will affect five million people in the United States.

As many as one in seven will die from this disease.

This was exactly what I wanted Rachel to comprehend. Though I'd read this statistic many times, seeing it in bold print, watching it with my daughter beside me, galvanized the high mortality rate. Our shoulders caved in upon one another as we watched in somber silence.

Greenfield's narrative focused on four women she filmed from early morning weigh-in and vital signs check through meals, treatment sessions, smoke breaks, and family phone calls. Their pain vibrated in every scene. It hurt to watch the bitter emotional wars that the four women waged with themselves, their families, the other patients, and the staff. I am certain the highly regarded Renfrew Centers save countless lives but I couldn't send Rachel there. It seemed far too combative and the outcomes for these four women looked grim.

This could have been Greenfield's editorial take on her experience, or was gentleness and recovery as meager as the meals the women pushed away? Were the rules at other centers as rigid as the ones displayed on Renfrew dining room walls? I imagined entering a dining room where signs read that only one napkin could be used and backpacks couldn't be worn. I'd have walked my rebellious butt straight out the front door. I assumed the one-napkin rule was enforced so women couldn't sneak the food into extra ones and then hide them in their backpacks. Rachel didn't do that stuff—she flat out refused to eat larger portions. She didn't hide a damn thing. Or so I thought.

Once the film ended, Rachel said what I was thinking. "It looked horrible there, Mom. I could never be in a place where everyone seemed so mean."

We hugged, that gesture so missed in our long-distance life, and her Burberry perfume floated into my next breath. I guaranteed her that if she ever needed a residential program we'd find a different kind.

"Mom," she asked. "Can we start looking online now? Maybe it won't come to this, but if it does, I can't go to one of those big places. I'd only go somewhere small, someplace that feels like home."

Home, I felt, hadn't worked all that well considering we had a skeletal daughter. No, wherever Rachel might go would need to feel like our home, only function a tad better. As Rachel willingly studied residential sites, as she spoke emphatically about recovery, I caught her words like a desert sucking spring rain. This killer of an illness would be survivable. We'd be the lucky ones and emerge from it in just a few months. I had to nail this certainty; otherwise Rachel would smell my fear and absorb it as hers.

During her week's vacation, anorexia didn't always command the stage. Rachel visited friends, talked on the phone with Mike, helped around the house, and took every opportunity to discuss her students and friends in Santa Rosa. She remained warm and genuine but once we sat at the dinner table, reality overcame us.

The night we watched *Thin*, I wore the mantle of Rachel's anorexia on my weary shoulders. Somehow, Mark and I had done all the wrong things and caused Rachel's illness. He'd carped about my weight; I'd either yelled back like a banshee or slunk off in a wounded silence. Maybe Mark had expected too much of her academically. Maybe she'd learned from me that going to the gym fixed everything. And together, perhaps we hadn't supported her enough when she had worried about her height. Or when people around her had died.

This is the mind game parents play in the middle of a starless night when morning is an eon away. These are the words you whisper back and forth, this *where did we go wrong?* Was it your fault? Or mine? You remember the words of an old friend, who said in an awkward sense of compassion, *Oh, I can see how this could happen in your house. You two are so careful about what you eat and how you exercise.*

Oh my God, was she right?

And then you hate yourselves because you didn't act sooner. Because you fell for the great Christmas miracle, and you didn't visit Santa Rosa enough after all, and you didn't make your daughter start treatment months ago. And three weeks earlier in New Jersey you didn't force her to start a residential program. And then you remember that your daughter is an adult who had for too long refused counseling. That legally you couldn't drag her there, and if somehow you had, and she resented it, perhaps that wouldn't have helped either.

The blame game isn't played in families when a child is newly diagnosed with a serious medical condition. Instead friends and neighbors rally with lasagnas and offer to walk the dog. There is empathy, and often that unspoken sense of feeling terrible for that family yet grateful your own child is well. I know that mindset; I've baked the casseroles and walked the dogs, said my prayers for the sick child and been thankful for Mike and Rachel's good health.

But when your daughter has anorexia, an illness both physical and psychological, you feel isolated and culpable. There aren't any casseroles; when you meet the gaze of someone asking how your daughter is, you think you see criticism in their eyes.

As a nurse I'd seen the countless ways illness affected a family. Invariably, it intensified any existing stress, and let's face it, what family doesn't have stress? I'd also seen the martyr effect, one parent taking on yeomen responsibility for the ill child or young adult. Sometimes that parent had no choice, other times it gave him or her a sense of control in a time without it. But martyrs belong only in Heaven; on earth they piss everyone off. No, I couldn't martyr myself.

Given my marriage to a crazed runner who too often commented on what he viewed as my weight problem, homicide wouldn't work either. Everything was going wrong for us. We worked too many hours, Fran had cancer, Rachel had a profound eating disorder, and Mike, the one who brought balance and levity to our group, lived twenty-five hundred miles away. We should have imploded. But in this most trying time of our marriage, Mark and I discovered something we'd never fully considered.

No one, no friend, no relative, no therapist could better understand how we felt.

No one knew my pain the way he did.

No one knew his pain as I did.

We clung together at night, such closeness a respite exceeding anything we'd experienced before. As we were getting the idea that times would worsen before they'd ever improve, we knew we'd get through them together. Oh, the menorah-tossing bride had come a long way.

On the night we watched *Thin*, Rachel fell asleep listening to hip-hop, the music of her soul. Mark and I settled down in bed with our books and one another. But we couldn't read. "She looks terrible," he said. "What if this outpatient program doesn't work?"

I repeated all those positive words Rachel's therapists had used but they sounded flat and unpromising to us. As we whispered into the night, Bentley whacked his tail against our bedroom wall. Dog hymns to keep us company.

The next morning, yoked like oxen, we shared the load and kept on going.

I'm not an innocent who thinks angels hover around waiting to protect us or, if all else fails, whisk us off to one of Heaven's better neighborhoods. I follow the daily news so I know for a fact that angels are in short supply. Yet I'm not entirely cynical. I recognize that if you're lucky, perhaps not angels, but the right people appear and extend a much-needed hand. One came our way.

It seemed that Rachel's nurse practitioner at her primary care office had little to offer other than monitoring Rachel's weekly labs and vital signs. I asked the office manager if any other doctors or nurse practitioners had experience treating patients with eating disorders and she said, "Not really." I explained what she no doubt already knew, how dire Rachel's condition had become and that I thought I should switch her to another practice. The office manager perked right up and agreed that it would definitely be a good idea. Generally one works hard to retain patients rather than pass them off, so I knew Rachel should be on her way to another practice. Immediately.

I called Rachel's therapist and left her a message to please call back as soon as possible. It was my day off and I sat in the living room, couch surfing more residential eating disorder programs. Early spring sunlight spilled across the walls that we had, in haste, painted a color called "autumn wheat." Once we got past the drama of saturated color instead of the white paint we'd always used, we liked how the room softly glowed. Now I needed that room to abate my bleakness.

Abigail called within the hour and how I appreciated that lifeline. I explained the primary care situation and she suggested another office.

"Dr. Nathan is with an alternative clinic," she said in her grounding voice. "But he's very reputable and has experience dealing with eating disorders. You should check out his website. Unfortunately, this practice won't accept Rachel's insurance. I'm not sure she could afford the fees on her AmeriCorps salary."

"We'll cover it. How do you think Rachel is doing? When she was home last week all our meals were brutal. And she's much thinner than before. If that's even possible."

"I know Rachel is making you and Mark quite anxious, but we think she's making progress. She's so motivated to get better. I speak with her nutritionist each week and we're sure she's about to have her a-ha moment. Give this a little more time."

I told Abigail that I'd be out in a few weeks. She offered that Rachel and I would meet with her for a joint session and I thanked her. I couldn't have asked for a kinder, more receptive therapist. Still, Rachel kept losing weight.

Next, I viewed the website for the alternative care center. Yes, I thought. Counseling. Massage. Yoga. Acupuncture. Reiki. I value compassionate care and a place where body and mind can be treated in unison. However, I hoped that Dr. Nathan had a degree in medicine as opposed to transcendental meditation. After Googling him, I lit up like the glowing walls that surrounded me. This physician had Mark's same academic credentials. His residency training had been rock solid and knowing how well traditional medicine and alternative modalities blend, I called for an immediate appointment. I don't think I sounded rude or pushy, just frantic, fretful, and even begging.

"My daughter could keel over tomorrow." I told the receptionist. "She's that sick, but denies it. She's working full-time and can't stay out of the gym."

"Of course," the receptionist said. "We'll get her right in this week. Don't worry about the insurance problem. We'll work everything out at her first appointment."

The autumn wheat room, those hands reaching out to catch me, made my day off. Tomorrow I'd be back at work and extend my own hand.

"You'll never believe this," Rachel said a week later. "Dr. Nathan is great! Before moving to Santa Rosa he directed the Cornell Inpatient Eating Disorders Program in New York. The man knows his stuff."

Bingo, I thought. "What did he tell you?"

"He said I'm medically stable. It's safe for me to work. However, if my weight doesn't improve I may need to work half-days. And maybe enter a treatment center. He'll work closely with Abigail. I signed a HIPAA form and he's happy to speak with you."

She'd meet weekly with Dr. Nathan and he'd monitor her weight, vital signs, and lab values. I spoke with Dr. Nathan later that day and he didn't talk about the ah-ha moment. From his experience he felt that Rachel, though clearly benefiting from her outpatient program, had lost so much weight that it was highly unlikely she'd regain it without the intensive support of a hospital program or residential treatment center. He suggested that we make arrangements now, and if we liked, he'd work with Cornell and have her admitted there. I asked when she should go and he felt that she could finish out the semester, but if anything changed, to be prepared for an immediate admission. He wanted to know if we had contacted any centers yet.

"I've been speaking with admissions people at centers around the country," I said. "Rachel knows this. She says we won't need it, but Mark and I know that she will."

"Good. I think she'll need residential treatment in another month or so."

Every doctor should be as compassionate over the phone as Dr. Nathan. I didn't feel rushed. Or like some stranger on the other side of the country. I felt listened to and then responded to. And most of all, he'd set a course for us. We had direction.

We'd narrowed our search to the Remuda Ranch in Arizona, Monte Nido in Oregon, and the Center for Hope of the Sierras in Nevada. I knew many fine programs existed but these were the ones Rachel connected with. Though she admired their professionalism, mission statements, and programs, she remained disengaged. "Not to worry," she said; any day she'd be gaining weight. I should believe that.

The last time I believed that our so-called Christmas miracle did not pan out.

Now I believe in biology. I knew that the prefrontal cortex, the brain structure responsible for planning and solving problems, doesn't reach full maturity until the midtwenties. Add an anorexic brain to that and I knew Rachel's belief systems and decision-making would be skewed. She'd most likely remind us yet again that as an adult, her treatment choices were hers. Legally she had a point; medically and ethically, we did.

How serendipitous, I told Mark, to find a Dr. Nathan in Santa Rosa. We'd been waiting for someone like him. Perhaps the Christmas miracle had happened now, but differently: instead of that quick fix, and who doesn't like the quick and easy cure, we'd been given the people to help Rachel do the hard work and cure herself. Thanks to the stars, the universe, karma, or God, we'd received a blessing. The way things were going we'd need plenty more.

Chapter Ten

California, 2007

Wearing only a pair of unmatched socks and lace-trimmed black panties, I stood in the locker room of a Santa Rosa gym. Two women walked into my aisle, banged open lockers, and began shucking their clothes. Soon we were all mostly naked together and I don't do group naked well. I turned my back to them and shimmied into my yoga pants.

"John is being transferred to a state prison," one of them said. "I'm terrified. Anything could happen to him there."

Her friend didn't respond. I finished dressing for my workout, sat down on the metal bench, and sipped my first coffee of the day. Rachel and I had left her house at dawn. She was already powering the elliptical machine but I could hardly power myself that April morning.

Finally the other woman spoke. "Well, I know you're frightened," she said with a fair amount of condescension, "but this may be a good place for him. He'll get help. Maybe even learn a trade. And I'm sure that the guards watch the prisoners well."

I didn't view prison life that way. I glanced at them to see how this comment landed. The worried woman edged closer to her friend but the friend backed away. "Things happen all the time in prison," she said. "I can't stand the thought of someone hurting John. What if he's attacked? Raped?"

"John committed a felony and should be in prison. I'm sorry to say that but it's true."

As I put my sneakers on, I wondered how the worried woman and John were related. Was he brother, friend, or partner? Coffee in hand, I walked past the two women. I wanted to hug the anxiety-wracked woman and say hey, I understand; my uncle did a fifteen-year stretch at Attica Correctional Facility, one of the toughest maximum security prisons in the country.

However, being hugged by a stranger you've just seen undressed may seem like a come-on rather than a kindness, so I did nothing.

I was still thinking about prisoners as I went to join Rachel. My mother had compassion for her older alcoholic brother. "Alcoholism is an illness," she always told me. I remember my uncle's gravelly voice when he played with me, but my father recalled a drunk who stole the wedding gifts soon after my parents had received them. My cousin said that my uncle had "bopped someone on the head." One isn't sent up the Chemung River to Attica in Upstate New York for ripping off a few toasters. And I bet that bop on the head caused a few skull fractures but as our family liked to gild the truth with cosmetics, I never learned my uncle's exact crime.

And yet my mother, imbued with empathy, also worried that her brother would suffer in prison. During his Attica years, my uncle called home on major holidays. These calls interrupted our celebrations like thunderstorms at a family picnic. Soon after talking with him, my mother and my aunt developed twin migraines. My mother hated pain and would share her "goodies" from her prescribed stash of Demerol and Valium. My aunt, the one without the addictive personality, would open her clenched fists and take respite. But then she'd close them. However, my mother's hands stayed open for the arsenal of pills legally prescribed by doctors month after month in a most polite doctor-patient exchange.

Family history weighed on me as I entered the gym floor and stepped on the elliptical by Rachel.

"Hi Mom," she said as I punched my age, weight, and projected time into the console. Rachel faced me, her expression grim. "It's okay if you work out beside me," she said. "But don't stare at how long I've been on the machine. Or how fast I'm going. My nutritionist says I can do a full forty-five-minute workout. I know that upsets you, but I promise I won't do a minute more. I won't do less either."

Oh, how we read each other.

"Don't nag me," Rachel said before I could. The elliptical lacked an icon to press the fear level but I lived at the highest one. The fluorescent lights of the industrial-designed gray and white room illuminated her face in stark relief, and in this unforgiving light I saw the lanugo of anorexia, the soft hair grown in a futile attempt at preserving body heat. Rachel's stork legs beat up and down in tune to her internal metronome, one even more intense than the techno music pulsating through the vast machine-filled room. Rachel's expression changed from grim to blank; only her exercise mattered at that moment. Like John, my uncle, and even my mother cradling her stash with tremulous fingers, Rachel was imprisoned.

Side by side, healthy mother and ill daughter, I thought about how I'd influenced Rachel regarding exercise. Despite the growing body of research indicating that parents *don't* cause anorexia, I still felt culpable about how I may have influenced her.

I first joined a gym in 1973. One year out of college, I worked as a nurse in my hometown hospital but I also had a part-time job as a rink guard, a job akin to a lifeguard only on ice. One afternoon following a five-hour skating shift in frostbite weather, I stopped at a new gym adjacent to the rink. One of the trainers challenged me to enter the weight room. I hesitated. No way did I want to be around grunting, smelly men. Besides, my arms were neither muscled nor tattooed. I'd never fit in but at the trainer's urging, I gave it a try.

Within a few weeks weight lifting had become my chamomile tea. I'd inherited my father's muscle and I kept getting stronger. Fueled with endorphins, I sailed through my nursing shifts, and years later through part-time work and motherhood. With a different drive I might have monitored my food intake, taken dietary supplements, worked with trainers, and competed in bodybuilding. But my drive stopped for pizza on the way home from the gym, and flaunting my muscle definition didn't appeal to me.

I kept weights by our television and used them while watching a show. Exercise addiction? No. I'd inherited something else from Dad. Narcolepsy. Sitting down at the wrong time of day or after a large meal made me sleepy. Once in college I'd pitched out of my first-row seat in an overcrowded organic chemistry lecture. Far more entertaining to the other students than the Krebs cycle, I got up off the floor uninjured but mortified.

So weights kept me awake when the kids were young and watching *Sesame Street* and especially, *Mr. Roger's Neighborhood*. Both Mike and Rachel had their own blue and pink two-pound dumbbells and we'd "work out" together. Later they played in the five-year-old soccer program, followed by elementary school basketball. Mark often coached their teams and perhaps too often, overcoached them. How quickly time passed, and soon high school hockey, skiing, snowboarding, lacrosse, and mountain biking consumed our days.

I continued at the gym but also bought an inexpensive young horse from a bride who wanted a new couch instead of a sweet mare. I squeezed in barn time whenever I could. Never a natural rider, I simply embodied Winston Churchill's quote, "There is something about the outside of a horse that's good for the inside of a man." And a woman.

Mark ran almost daily, as this mattered to the inside of him. On the weekends we took family hikes and I'd watch Mark with the kids and I'd think how lucky we were. Like most of my friends who were pediatric nurses, gratitude came easily to me. A walk in the woods meant as much as a summer vacation.

But were we excessive with exercise? Maybe. One month after his fiftieth birthday Mark completed the Vermont City Marathon though he had a stress fracture in his leg. When my hands turned into lobster claws due to advanced Lyme disease, I covered my intravenous antibiotic line with an ace bandage and went to the barn. Strong teeth helped me adjust my horse's bridle and tighten the girth of her saddle.

Was this good role modeling? Depends on whom you ask. An Olympian would say we taught our kids to keep going, to walk off pain, injuries, and illnesses. A psychologist might counter that we put unrealistic demands on ourselves and taught the kids to do the same. Either way, both Mike and Rachel absorbed our notions that exercise ranked with oxygen.

Mike took a fifty-mile bike ride on the morning of his high school AP Biology exam "to clear his head." He quipped that if he hadn't learned the material by now, why bother. I'd known how much preparation he'd done in the weeks before. *He* was the one I thought might be obsessive about school and sports, but he sanely balanced both. As for Rachel, she didn't obsess about sports as a teenager. Yes, she liked playing hockey but if the girls lost a game, she recovered after a team dinner at the Olive Garden. She enjoyed doing yoga with me but during more intense work, she slipped into child's pose and took a rest. Though she liked skiing on what passed for powder in Vermont, she headed to the lodge for soup and hot chocolate after her fourth run.

Rachel's easygoing approach to exercise seemed healthy. I assumed she'd keep this attitude, as if the cement of her personality had been laid down forever. I forgot how cement cracks.

Those first cracks were tiny fissures that went unnoticed.

During Rachel's junior year in college Mark and I took his parents and

Rachel on a vacation to the Lawrence Welk Resort in San Diego. Mike sounded relieved when he said he couldn't get time off from work and we joked about the upcoming week of "champagne music." To the grandparents this would be the stardust of halcyon days but to me it would be slow torture.

The resort gym was a champagne-music-free zone. Each day we saw the same woman working out there. We tried not staring and I noticed others averting their eyes as well. The woman, perhaps in her midthirties, had scant brown hair clipped close to her head. Too much sun had scarred her tan face. Eyes downcast, she worked the elliptical machine as if her life depended on it. Profoundly thin and chained to that machine, she never spoke or acknowledged anyone.

"How can she be that way?" Rachel asked after we'd first seen her.

"It's a sickness," I said. "No doubt she can't help herself."

"How scary."

For breakfast that morning we had the requisite bagels and lox. But then we added fruit, omelets, and cereal; no one should ever be hungry at a mostly Jewish table. Fran and Joe planned a shopping outlet trip, Mark thought he'd read medical journals on the sunny deck chair, and Rachel and I opted for pool time. After tidying the condo kitchen we changed into our swimsuits and as we stood in the hallway, Fran gave us a long, hard stare. Those looks never boded well.

Body shaming. How many guises it comes under. I braced myself for Fran's assessment of me. Over the years I'd heard how my legs were heavier than hers. She'd always been bigger in the bust than me, but alas, I had larger hips. (No doubt they match my legs!) I'd put on a few; she never gained an ounce. My responses stayed consistent. But this time, Fran stared at Rachel. "Your cheeks have gotten so round," she said and then tweaked Rachel's face. "You were such a skinny Minnie [a Fran compliment of the highest order]. But you've put on some weight. How much do you weigh now?"

Rachel burned crimson.

"Her weight is perfect!" I snapped back.

And it was. I should have taken my mother-in-law aside and said how damaging her comments could be. Instead I coldly said that we needed to leave for the pool. On the way there, I reminded Rachel that yes, her weight was perfect and she looked beautiful. And we'd known her grandmother to be rude in the past. Just let it go. I did. My parents had raised me with their archaic sense of manners. One must be polite at all costs to older adults and in-laws. You could think whatever appropriate or highly inappropriate things you wanted but your first amendment right did not include "talking back" to the elders.

Two minutes later I dove into that overchlorinated pool while the Lennon Sisters warbled in the background. Lap after lap, I swam off my anger. Rachel sunned her hurt feelings on a teak lounge chair and then joined me to play like baby seals as we'd done years before.

At that time I didn't connect the different prisons we inhabited. Mark's harsh relationship with food and exercise, Fran's obsession and frequent unsolicited commentary about weight, my uncle's Attica years, my mother's prescription addiction, and even my stoic acceptance of *okay, life is hard, go work it off*. But we were all stuck one way or another. Nor did I read how those generational stories were unfolding, and how they even linked to that emaciated woman on the elliptical. Never did I imagine that one day, I'd be working out next to a girl, *my girl*, as ravaged as her.

Twenty minutes on an April morning in the Santa Rosa gym with Rachel finished me. "I can't do this," I told her. "I can't watch you any longer."

Rachel looked surprised. "Mom, how can you say that? You love being at the gym. We've always had such a good time working out together."

"I don't care what your nutritionist says. You shouldn't be here. Watching you terrifies me."

The techno music blaring through the gym felt like a dystopian soundtrack in a robotic world dominated by steel gray machines. Rachel looked my way and apologized for ruining my time. She thought I'd be happier if I went upstairs to the yoga room for a short practice. I agreed but once I got there, I couldn't focus and the harder I tried, the more frozen my breath became. In yoga, we tend to get closer to our emotions, and sometimes, when that cuts too much, it's best to roll up your mat and walk away.

I did just that. I returned to the locker room, didn't even bother changing my clothes, and left with my gym bag. My world had unraveled yet the outside one carried on. We'd parked in a small strip mall and how normal the people looked as they entered Starbucks. Like in a fairy tale, once upon a time that had been my life too. Rachel had the car keys, so I sat on the curb and waited for the sun to thaw my cold dread. Normally so private and controlled in public, I dropped my face into my hands and cried. I felt more naked than I did standing in my unmatched socks.

But unlike the locker-room woman, the one worried about John, who went untouched in her sadness, I soon felt a hand on my shoulder. Rachel caressed my back and her woodsy sweet Burberry perfume filled the space between us. I couldn't speak. She huddled beside me and we wept together.

"I'm sorry," she gasped. "I hate what I'm doing to you and Dad."

I'd lost trust in the words describing Rachel's treatment. Words like *a-ha moment* and *any day she'll turn things around*. Instead, I saw Rachel in a desperate free fall, and therapy merely a resting place before she crashed. If I talked to her now about increasing calories and reducing exercise it would be like dousing a California wildfire with a squirt gun. But I believed in the word *sorry*, a word encompassing so much.

I hugged Rachel and her bones felt like honeycombs. "I know you are, honey," I said. "Let's get the hell out of here."

A few days later I flew home. Long-distance parenting by phone proved almost futile. I'd be back in California in two weeks.

Chapter Eleven

California, 2007

A battered wooden rocker anchored the corner of the first-grade classroom. I'd spent countless hours in similar rockers, first rocking babies as a teenage babysitter and later as a nurse and a mother. That old rocker on the edge of a frayed and faded oriental rug felt like comfort food to me, the Friday afternoon guest reader.

"Read a Clifford book," Luis pleaded.

"Clifford, Clifford!" echoed his classmates.

Most of Rachel's students were born in California but many of their parents weren't documented. The kids worried about their parents being taken away. And sometimes they worried about drive-by shootings. No wonder they latched onto this gigantic red dog capable of saving any day.

Late afternoon light saturated the room. Eighteen kids sat "crisscross applesauce" on the rug facing me, often creeping closer to my rocker. I'd glance up while reading so I could check my audience response. Once I caught Rachel wobbling to her desk. She grabbed a corner for support and then chugged a Diet Coke. It looked like she wouldn't faint so I kept reading.

Earlier that day during recess, Rachel's supervising teacher had stopped me on the playground. We sat down at a child-sized picnic table and I struggled to tuck my long legs underneath. "Now that it's hot," Clare said. "I'm afraid Rachel will faint out here."

I tried reassuring both of us that at least she kept well hydrated.

"I'm glad you're here," she said. "Rachel has been so excited about your trip. And it's fine if you come to school with her. We can always say you're a volunteer."

"Thanks. I'm not sure what Rachel has told you, but she's been attending an outpatient treatment program for a few months. Mark and I don't see any improvement and we're trying to convince her to enter a residential center."

"Thank God. We're all terrified for her. I'll do everything I can in terms of negotiating her AmeriCorps contract." Clare paused. "And I know all about interventions," she confided. "My husband needed one a while ago."

"I think," I said with utter faith, "it won't come to that. I'm almost certain she'll enter treatment willingly."

Clare looked across the hot asphalt playground to where Rachel had organized a game of tag. "She's amazing with the kids. She loves them and they love her right back. It's hard seeing her this way."

I wiggled my toes to keep the circulation going in my cramped legs. They couldn't be numb in case I needed to sprint to Rachel if the heat did her in. Her students thought I came to school to play hula-hoop or read with them. They didn't know I came to watch over her. So I needed Clifford as much as they did and being the Friday afternoon guest reader lifted the pall off my days.

As I read a few Clifford books to my wiggly but attentive group, the magic of children's literature dropped fairy dust on me too so I could believe in happy endings. I finished my reading just as the school bell sounded at 3 p.m. Amid their crescendo of glad-it's-Friday voices, the kids gathered their backpacks, gave us hugs, and ran to the door. After the last child had left, I handed Rachel a container of Dannon fat-free eighty-five calorie yogurt like the one she'd had at breakfast and lunch. Never did she pass up yogurt.

For breakfast I'd made scrambled eggs with Vermont cheddar cheese and turkey bacon. I'd buttered toast and for ambience, I turned on the gas fireplace. Just back from the gym, Rachel kissed my cheek and slipped into a chair. "This looks so good," she said.

I'd divided the eggs and bacon equally, hoping that as she chatted she'd simply forget to restrict her intake. This was like expecting that someone with a flight phobia would ignore the takeoff thanks to a friendly conversation about the weather. Rachel parsed her food, eating one toddler-sized bite at a time. I recalled Mark's words before leaving home. *Just because you're trying to be a good role model for Rachel doesn't mean you gain weight! Don't eat like an animal out there.*

Telling Mark that I was a size 8 and not exactly large was like telling the phobic flier that once that plane took off, landing was even more fun. Wasted words. I'd picked the scabbed wound of his criticism that morning and packed my suitcase.

As Rachel toyed with her plate, I recalled how she'd heard Mark's conversations. *Nancy. Look at all the fat and cholesterol you're eating.* He'd admire his grilled chicken and bright green broccoli florets done al dente with a mere pinch of olive oil and say *now this is a heart-healthy dinner.* Keeping quiet through too many meals and public health bulletins, I'd unwittingly substituted authentic peace with silence. But all along, Rachel absorbed her father's words into her own unspoken lexicon.

Mike thrived by ignoring Dr. Heart Healthy. While still living at home, and rocking his chair at the dinner table, he'd laugh and say, "Dad, you're going overboard. Simmer down. Mom isn't eating that much." Mike, confident in his genial independence, didn't give a rat's ass about his dad's nutritional advice. Having Mike at the table neutralized the country of careful eating and plain old eating. Without him at the table, Rachel was pinioned between the two parents she was both devoted to, and yet tormented by.

It didn't surprise me to see Rachel shoulder her first graders' problems. She did the same thing with us. She'd borne too much weight at our family table and finally had collapsed beneath it. Now she couldn't eat those damn cage-free hormone-free eggs scrambled with her favorite cheddar cheese. I'd had a sleepless night after our right-out-there-on-the-curb cry and now I needed food. As she nibbled her eggs, I decimated mine along with my bacon, her bacon, two containers of those teeny-weeny blueberry yogurts, toast, and an oversized glass of orange juice. I figured that as Rachel's anorexia bore on, our combined weight would be identical to pre-illness days. I'd be wearing more of it, and she profoundly less.

Rachel watched me *clean my plate* as my own parents had admonished. "I wish," she said in the way I talked about winning the lottery, "I could eat like you."

"Sweetie, once you did. And you were never overweight. Now you really need more calories for energy."

The teaspoon trembled in her hand and I guessed her shakes were due to low blood sugar. "I'm trying," she said while scooping out the last of the yogurt. "And when you're here I eat better than when you aren't."

"I can't imagine what that's like."

Rachel smiled brightly as she switched subjects. "I have an idea. Let's go to Target after dinner so I can buy Dad's birthday gift. Do you need anything?"

I needed so much but it wouldn't come from Target.

I needed to convince Rachel that her outpatient program had failed.

I needed her to understand that despite her normal lab values, her solid vital signs, and her still-monthly periods, she was headed for a physiologic crisis. She'd lost one-third of her weight and yet worked full-time, starting each day at the gym. And despite face-to-face contact with little kids, their runny noses, strep throats, and lingering hugs, she'd escaped illness her entire teaching year; healthier friends had succumbed along the way. I didn't know where her stamina came from but I needed to convince her that a body could be beaten only so far.

Even one as resilient as hers.

And I needed Rachel's therapist to comment on Rachel's size zero jeans, thinning hair, and facial lanugo. I needed her to say, *Now is the time for more aggressive treatment.*

However, I had no idea what sitting down with a therapist entailed. Chances are I needed one myself, but like my riding friends, we said our horses were our shrinks. Sometimes after a good ride, we horse ladies would kvetch about whatever ailed us. Generally that worked, but now I had more troubles than a horse or a friend could fix.

Therefore, I looked forward to meeting a real therapist who'd say, *Time's up Rachel. Your life is at stake.*

The counseling center covered two floors of an old downtown red brick building appearing solid enough to withstand earthquakes and floods. Rachel's young therapist, Abigail, welcomed us into her small office. Tall windows overlooked the parking lot and beyond that, the mountains. Craggy ridges burnished purple in the late day and grounded me like my mountains did at home. Abigail emanated a gentle spirit with her low, warm voice and easy smile. Within minutes we had hot tea in our hands as we discussed my trip to Santa Rosa as well as Rachel's week at school, the gym, and the kitchen table. Rachel spoke about positive changes but also about her ongoing challenges.

"Perhaps," Abigail said, "you could be quite specific about these issues."

Rachel shared the good news. She'd been able to restrict her daily workouts to forty-five minutes. As for nutrition, she was still eating eggs, yogurts, salads, veggies, fruits, and grilled chicken and fish. Unfortunately, no luck with adding bread, potatoes, or even pizza back to her diet.

"How do you feel about increasing your portion sizes?" Abigail asked.

"Very anxious," Rachel said.

I didn't hear anxiety. I heard certainty and that voice said, *No way will I eat more food*. Abigail might not have heard her the way I did.

"I understand," Abigail nodded. "I recognize this fear but I know you can conquer it. I spoke with your nutritionist a few days ago and Tom's impressed with your desire to recover. He thinks you'll be adding larger portions and more food groups any day. He said you and your mom will be having dinner with him tonight."

"We'll have a great time," Rachel said enthusiastically. "My mom loves Mexican food. She lived in New Mexico and we grew up eating enchiladas." Again, Rachel had deflected the conversation.

I wouldn't. "Actually, I think Rachel is restricting more than she did a few weeks ago. Maybe this dinner will be good because she loves enchiladas too." My subtext meant that I wanted Tom to evaluate Rachel's eating, to see her circle her empty fork through those enchiladas that were once one of her favorite dishes.

Abigail smiled with empathy. Support. I knew she meant well. "This must be hard for you as a mother," she said so appropriately.

Hard?

Hard for me meant living cross-country from an ill daughter. Hard meant caring professionally for children with uncontrolled epilepsy, brain tumors, genetic disorders, or lifelong damage from violence and abuse. Hard meant feeling the same fear their parents did. But hard couldn't begin to describe the feral looks in their eyes and in mine. However, for the sake of this session not floating out to a melodramatic sea, I leaned forward, dug the chewed-off nails on my right hand into my left palm, and said, "Yes, this is hard."

I explained that I'd feel better once Rachel gained weight. Rachel and Abigail nodded. We sipped our tea and I stared at the purple mountains. How beautiful the Sonoma Valley, the rich bounty of food and wealth for some, but for others, abject poverty, and for Rachel, starvation in the fertile land of plenty.

"It's difficult," Abigail offered, "to stand by and feel helpless. But just your being here is good for Rachel."

Abigail then addressed Rachel and reaffirmed how much she understood the struggle to eat. Yesterday, Abigail said, had been a bad day for her. She'd had a full day of graduate school followed by an evening of clients. She'd been tired but had to stop at the grocery store. However, before she could force herself to park and then buy food, she'd circled the parking lot twelve times. Finally she parked, shopped, and then went home and made dinner.

"It's good that you went into that grocery store," Rachel said. "You must be exhausted after such long workdays."

"I am, but I love my work."

"So do I," Rachel answered. "Some days I work ten hours but it's alright. The kids make everything worthwhile."

This mutually supportive, smiling camaraderie didn't include my main concern that each day Rachel dropped more weight. My inner self wanted to jump through my skin and scream, *What the fuck is going on here?*

"Each time I visit," I said in my fake voice, that calm, nonaggressive, nonthreatening one, "Rachel is thinner. I don't see any improvement even though I know how hard all of you are working together. How do you feel about residential programs?"

Abigail checked both Rachel's expression and mine. "Well sometimes they work," she hedged. "And they can be lifesaving, but often, the girls learn bad habits from one another. We're hoping that Rachel will turn this around soon and commit to real change. I think we can offer her a bit more time before considering residential care." She then spoke about her personal experience at an Arizona program and said that without it, she might not have gotten better.

I wondered about Abigail's recovery. Though her weight had normalized, she'd needed to cruise around a grocery store parking lot a dozen times before mustering up the resolve to go inside. Listening to her made me think this illness was one not fully recoverable. Is this why I flinched when I watched the documentary *Thin?* Yes, I'd judged the film too critically. Chances are the message had been that the eating disorder was the harsh place, not the actual treatment facility.

Abigail wanted Rachel to fully grasp the disease gripping them both. "This weekend," she said, "I'm going to a funeral for a friend I met in treatment."

"How awful," Rachel said and then offered minutes of support.

A fatality. My greatest fear. "I go nuts when my child has a prolonged seizure," a mother told me the week before. "Do you know what I worry about most with these long seizures?" Of course I did. When death thoughts linger on your mind, you know you've entered the uncharted territory of parenthood. And that mother and I were each struggling in its lost zone.

Twenty minutes later we finished our session with Abigail. As we drove away from that solid brick building, the distant mountains glowed in the deepening light. California looks washed out at midday but by evening, the sea, sky, and mountains are jewel-toned. A good backdrop for what I assumed wouldn't be the perfect dinner ahead.

I asked Rachel if her sessions were always like this and she said yes. She thought Abigail was an amazing therapist who so understood and supported her. With her, she never felt judged. I could see this.

"Abigail's eating disorder seems quite active," I said. "Hearing how she circled the supermarket surprised me."

"Well, Mom, Abigail articulated just how an anorexic feels. That's what you should understand. And I hope you listened carefully when she said I didn't need a residential program."

I was about to comment when Rachel practically rammed the car in front of us after the driver had braked for an intersection. "Shit!" I yelled. "Watch out." I grabbed the armrest and held it tight.

"It's that asshole driver, not me, that you should be yelling at!"

"Sweetie, just watch the traffic, okay?"

"Would you stop being so hyper? I know how to drive and you need to chill!"

So I chilled and settled in with my thoughts about the therapy session and the presence of Abigail's own devils. As nurses we understand that the patient is the one with the problem to be addressed. Our own waits back at home. I didn't think Abigail experienced enough yet to fully respect that boundary. Ruefully, I noticed something else. Rachel had shifted the focus of her eating disorder to Abigail. And when she talked about her dead friend, Rachel had provided utmost empathy. On one level, how sensitive of Rachel to consider Abigail's pain. But on another, Rachel had made a clean escape. She bore my own iron-cast shield: subtly turning the conversation away from self. She'd absorbed all her father's work ethic, perfectionism, and complex food habits, but from me, she'd learned the art of the emotional getaway.

As a young woman I'd worked for the Indian Health Service in Gallup, New Mexico. Here I found love for pediatric nursing, Native American culture, Southwestern sunsets, and New Mexican cuisine. Chicken enchiladas, chili rellenos, and honey-drenched sopapillas, all washed down with an icy Corona created heaven in my stomach. I'd seen scores of young children thrive on spicy food, so my babies weaned from breast milk to chili. Rachel warbled at age two in a rapid gibberish only Mike seemed to understand: *Ensalsaslas*, she'd sing out amid an incomprehensible sentence. Mike would easily translate that Rachel wanted enchiladas for dinner.

Would this be so tonight?

The taqueria bustled with Friday evening customers. In this Latine neighborhood, families with four or five children crowded around picnic tables both inside and out. Here friends met, kids yelled across tables, and the line cooks joked as they efficiently prepared their orders.

I admired my full plate as we sat outside, the fiery globe of California sun melting into the darkening mountains. Refried beans spilled across a hill of brown rice and three plump green chili enchiladas looked like the best thing I'd seen all day. Once this place might have been a culinary mecca for us but now Rachel faced her dinner like it was a mountain pass to cross in a blizzard.

Tom sat down with his own plate brimming with fine food. Earlier Rachel had mentioned Tom's counseling experience, his advanced degrees in nutrition and health, and I knew he'd be most helpful. A tall, affable man in his midthirties, Tom asked about my trip and how I was doing. I filled him in fast and ended my spiel with the fact that Rachel kept losing weight.

Tom reiterated what Abigail had said. He seemed pleased that Rachel had shortened her daily workout time; he understood her ongoing challenges with larger portions and adding back foods she'd once liked.

Rachel noticed the portions on our plates. "You get your money's worth here," she said warily. "But everything is supersized and that can't be healthy."

"Not eating isn't so healthy either," I said.

"Mom," Rachel answered while splitting an enchilada into three pieces and braving a forkful, "when you talk so much about how I should be eating, it actually backfires, makes me eat less. I know I'm making you and Dad nervous but you really need to relax. You were crazy back there in the car."

"Just eat half an enchilada with some beans and rice. That would make me happy. And less crazy."

"Mom, you're pressuring me!"

"I don't mean to."

"I know that." Her anger ebbed. "I feel so guilty about what I'm doing to all of us. But I'm trying. Really."

"Guilt will wear you down. Just work on getting better."

Rachel ate a few more forkfuls of enchiladas and froze. Meal over. Tom didn't urge her to eat. He remained professional, nonjudgmental, and smiled often. It seemed that California therapists did a great deal of smiling and nodding. I longed to say, *Easy to be so congenial when it's not your daughter.*

Tom and I did a super job cleaning our plates. Though he watched Rachel carefully, he never commented on what she did or didn't do. Did he think I was intrusive and making it more difficult for Rachel to eat? But I felt that this meal was no worse, or better, than most of her other ones. And I wasn't around for the majority of them. Were Mark and I haunting her from afar? I hated thinking we were the root of her evil illness but this is how a parent thinks. However, at this point the major issue was Rachel's survival. Not guilt or blame. Just fighting anorexia harder than it fought us.

I had one well-considered question for Tom. "In your practice, how many women have you seen who lost as much weight as Rachel regain that weight in the outpatient setting?"

His answer came slowly. "Two," he said. "In the five years I've been doing this."

I thanked him. I'd awaited such a clear answer. Feeling better, I'd learned, didn't come from the cure alone. It also came from honest answers. Without telling us what to do, Tom let us know what needed doing. Rachel said nothing but her serious expression spoke for her.

We drove to Target after dinner with tension between us as tight as our seatbelts. I refrained from screaming, *You need residential care now.* Raw emotion from the shotgun seat rarely makes a trip safer. Instead I took a series of yoga breaths and focused on the shopping trip, something we'd liked doing since Rachel had been a two-year-old proudly carrying her pink plastic bedazzled purse. Yes, shopping would relax both of us. And for the next few hours we'd talk about anything besides food.

Once in Target we browsed the greeting cards aisle, looking for the perfect cards for Mark's birthday. Not finding the right ones, we quickly walked to the opposite end of the store to look at shoes. Nothing there of interest. Then Rachel bolted pell-mell across several garishly lit aisles to the electronics department in search of a Crosby, Stills, Nash & Young CD for Mark. Not finding what she wanted, Rachel took off once again for the greeting card aisle. This time we found something. Cards in hand, she left for the hair products aisle.

Finally I caught on. We were speed walking the store.

"Rachel," I said as she selected a shampoo even though she had more at home. "You're inventing things to shop for just so you can run around. This is madness! I'm going out to the car. You meet me when you're done."

"Oh all right," she growled. "You're being really pissy tonight."

Her words were a dozen bee stings. Rachel and Mike hadn't criticized me much when they were teenagers. They'd been far easier than I expected for kids that age. Mark and I had set a certain bar for them and they'd risen to it. There could be no drinking and driving whatsoever. No entering a car with someone who'd been drinking. No drugs. No disrespect for teachers, coaches, friends, each other, or for parents. And we needed updates as to where they were and whom they were with.

For such compliance, I didn't needle them about homework, bad language, or disgusting bedrooms. Nor were there curfews. Freedom came with huge responsibility but its lack held consequences they didn't want. My parents offered me this deal and a generation later, it still worked.

Rachel and I talked nonstop through her teenage years and had shared so many good conversations. We also practiced yoga, went shopping, and invariably stopped for coffee or lunch. No lack of appetites on our part. At the time, I admired Rachel's sense of self-esteem. So did her teachers and the parents of the kids she babysat for.

Still, one thing bothered Rachel and good talks couldn't alter it. Her height. The short, cute girls had boyfriends; she only had the desire for one. And though one came her way senior year, she still felt too tall.

I'd reassure her that one day, she'd be happy being tall. She'd see this as an asset rather than a liability. "Right," she'd say unconvincingly.

During all those good years we'd had conversations both wise and witty. Never had they held the high wattage that snapped between us now.

Once we were both back in the car, her bags full of things not needed, Rachel revved the engine and sped across the parking lot. Even at seventeen she'd been a safe driver. This new reckless driving angered me.

"I don't know who you are these days," I said bitterly. "You aren't the daughter I once knew!" Never had I said anything like this and I despised my words.

Rachel gripped the steering wheel and stared ahead. "I thought you'd be the last person to turn on me. Well guess what?" she asked in a voice so charged that a few more words would burn us, "I don't know who you are either!"

She'd called that right. I'd changed. Tense all day, awake at night, watching, always watching her eat, so focused on her illness that I'd overlooked the person with it and how that illness had changed her as well.

Mark and I didn't fully appreciate this change because we still viewed anorexia as a behavioral illness leading to a full-blown psychiatric disorder. Unfortunately, anorexia is also the story of a beautiful brain, its structure and function, damned by starvation. So many aspects of Rachel's personality spun out of her control. It must have taken a herculean effort to teach, but those kids kept her going. They must have dangled steel threads for her to grip as she leaned over to help them with a spelling word.

Dr. James Greenblatt, a board certified child and adult psychiatrist and the chief medical officer at Walden Behavioral Care Center in Walden, Massachusetts, writes clearly and chillingly about the effects of anorexia on the brain. Greenblatt states, "Studies using computerized tomography (CT) and magnetic resonance imaging (MRI) to view the brain have found that young women with anorexia have reduced brain mass."[5]

He explains the consequences. "Those with anorexia often have cognitive problems relating to attention, concentration, memory, and visuospatial ability."

According to his research, long-term weight recovery reverses some but not all the changes both on brain structure and in cognition.

Greenblatt also describes the role of serotonin, a neurotransmitter substance allowing neurons to communicate with one another. In anorexia, patients have decreased serotonin and MRI studies have indicated that there are also decreased receptors for this neurotransmitter. The direct result of lowered serotonin is deregulation of appetite, mood, and impulse control. Medications, Greenblatt writes, are not the right answer. Immediate improved and lasting nutrition is.

Deregulation of appetite, mood, and impulse control? Those words define how Rachel had changed. Naturally the information we need is not always available when first needed. It would be months before Mark and I understood some of the complex brain mechanisms affected by anorexia. Expecting an aha moment of epiphany was like me asking one of my patients having a grand mal seizure to please stop shaking and not do it again.

However, on the long day culminating in a rare, but for us, vicious argument, Rachel and I practiced the humbling art of the apology. Yes, we'd both changed but not completely.

"I've been a jerk," I said as we sat on her couch that evening. I brushed strands of wispy hair from her angular face. "I'm sorry."

Rachel put her stick arm around me and smiled faintly. "We were both jerks. And I'm just as sorry."

After Rachel fell asleep that night I called Mark. Now midnight on the East Coast, Mark and Bentley were getting ready for bed. I described our day.

"I can just see Rachel counseling the therapist," Mark said. "So how are you doing?"

"I'm frazzled."

"Is your asthma okay? Are you coughing?"

"No. Just tired. Very tired."

Mark said that he and Bentley were lonely without me. "Bentley," Mark added, "tell Nancy how much we miss her and wish she could be home." I heard the repetitive thump of a fanned-out golden retriever tail against our pine bed.

"Love you," Mark whispered and I said "I love you too." How hard for families to battle illness if the parents are missing such love. With our love, and a good dog, Mark and I could wage one hell of a fight.

A few hours later I lay awake. I'd checked Rachel's pulse before she fell asleep and then checked it later. Each time it remained between thirty-four and thirty-six beats per minute. A slowed heart rate is a hallmark of anorexia. Each beat of her threatened heart was a bead on my rosary, one more prayer, so many yet ahead. Once during the long night she woke and felt my hand on her wrist.

"Am I dying?" she whispered. "Is my heart stopping?"

"Of course not. If your heart had stopped you wouldn't be talking. You're fine, sweetie. Go back to sleep." I rubbed her bony spine as gently as possible until she slept. I finished my rosary while imagining cardiac abnormalities and asystole, the melodic word meaning "no heart rate."

The next morning, a Saturday, brought cool Northern California fog, time for strong coffee and the warmth of the gas fireplace. Rachel ate yogurt and I of course, much more. Always an early riser, she was up before her housemates so I cornered her. "Rachel," I begged. "Why don't you go to a residential program now? You know you'll need to eventually and we could get the whole process started while I'm here."

"Mom, you need to back off," she said like a teacher patiently telling a first grader that she couldn't go to the playground and please don't ask again. "You didn't hear Abigail saying that. Besides, Dr. Nathan says I'm stable. I still have a few weeks left on my teaching contract. I refuse to break that and end the semester early."

"Your school would understand."

"Look, I'll think about one of those places once school is over. Maybe you could stay out here until then. We could start the Maudsley program right here in Santa Rosa."

A few weeks earlier I'd finished Laura Collins's powerful book *Eating with Your Anorexic: A Mother's Memoir* (McGraw Hill, 2004). This book details the Maudsley Approach or Family-Based Treatment (FBT) first begun at the Maudsley Hospital in London.

In this treatment plan, adolescents remain at home and their parents take complete responsibility for ensuring their adequate nutrition. Ideally the family is involved with a team of therapists well educated in this approach. Early studies in both the short term and long term are promising. I liked the premise of the parents remaining the primary caregivers in this illness, but the concern was the word *adolescent*. Nearly twenty-three, Rachel was, or so we thought, fully adult. At the time of her illness, there were no studies on how this program helped young adults, so Mark and I hesitated to bring Rachel home to try it. We also feared she had become too ill for a home-based program. If only we'd known about this the year before. If only we hadn't allowed Rachel to move to California. If only we'd said, *Screw the Christmas miracle; we'll start the Maudsley method*. But none of this happened.

Rachel had read portions of the book and thought we'd be ideal candidates. Rachel, who always had her family's back, appreciated the viewpoint that the families weren't the culprits in eating disorders and were instead a core part of the treatment plan. However, my doubts lingered.

"I'm not sure about this." I told her. "You aren't a teenager and so far there aren't many studies done on young adults. We don't have time to make mistakes. That's why I keep pushing for residential care. It's the safest place for you."

"I know you think that. I'd give anything to make you and Dad less anxious but I won't and I repeat, leave work yet. Please give me a few more weeks."

As always, we'd hit an impasse. If only she'd been fourteen and still living at home. If only.

That afternoon Rachel and I ate at a small café near her house. We'd eaten there when she'd first moved to Santa Rosa and on that day, she'd finished her salad and sandwich. Not so eight months later. Despite the cheerful yellow walls, the aroma of freshly brewed coffee, and the fact that we were in no hurry, Rachel stared miserably at her food. After ordering she'd agreed to eat half her grilled chicken sandwich, potato salad, and garden salad. But I couldn't nag her.

"Look how big these servings are," she said when the waitress served us.

"No they aren't," I countered.

Rachel ate one-quarter of the sandwich, nudged pieces of potato salad around her plate, and then munched on the lettuce. Forty-five minutes later I said we couldn't leave until she'd eaten what she'd said she would. No excuses.

The longer the food sat there, the more tense we became. Another fifteen minutes passed. The waitress asked if we needed anything; people at other tables watched us like we were a bad soap opera.

"Please," I said firmly. "You need the calories."

"I'm trying, Mom. I really am."

"Try harder. You can do it. I know you can."

"Mom, I hate how you worry, but I can't eat right now. Being here this long only makes it more impossible. I have a stomachache. And I'm getting a migraine."

Her irritation with me matched my frustration with her. Finally I exchanged our plates and plowed through her lunch as if I hadn't eaten in twelve hours. We went to the ladies room while waiting for the waitress to return the change from our bill. Once back at the table I noticed a small note tucked under Rachel's plate. I grabbed it before she returned. I had no idea who'd penned it, but if I had, that person, most likely a guy, would have heard my diatribe against his inexcusable insensitivity. And possible criminal intent.

"Call me for a hot date," the note read. A phone number was included. How cruel to leave this for one as gaunt and ravaged as she. I didn't tell Rachel about the note but I'd never forget it. She seemed numb to how desperate she appeared and never noticed those gawking while we ate. This had to be a comfort of sorts unless someone with a prey drive homed in on her. I recalled a beautiful dark-haired teenager I knew from the clinic. Due to her developmental differences and diagnosis, her mother worried how her trusting child could be taken advantage of. I knew her concern.

The next morning, as every morning, I found a better note, the one Rachel's housemate, Joy, left by my toothbrush. Folded in precise origami style, printed in small and tidy block letters, Joy left daily inspirational messages for both Rachel and me.

I remembered Sophie, Rachel's close college friend who'd lost her beloved boyfriend. How Rachel had cared for her, and now, Joy did the same for Rachel. Good karma and we needed all we could get.

In the past we'd laughed and chatted in so many coffee shops as we'd lingered over that second cup and those last morsels of muffins. I hoped these memories might encourage Rachel to eat *all* of something again. This particular coffee shop, built in a former downtown factory, had lofty ceilings, exposed brickwork, a dozen or so wooden tables, and plenty of room for the patrons. Some read newspapers; others worked on their laptops or played on their cell phones. No one seemed in a hurry. Love that laid-back California vibe.

"I've been coming here on weekends by myself," Rachel said with a sadness lacing her words tight. "I spend a few hours here and pick away at a muffin. I feel better being alone."

She'd never been a solitary person. "Have you told your therapist?" I asked.

"Yeah."

"Are you feeling depressed?"

She mulled that question over. "No. Not really. I'm just tired from school and working out. Once school is over, I'll be more rested. I'll eat better then."

"Why don't you forget school?" I urged again. "We can get you a bed at a treatment center today. You can't keep living like this."

Anger flared. "Absolutely not! I refuse to break my contract," she said as she had before. "Besides, my labs and vital signs are stable. Even Dr. Nathan says I can wait a few more weeks." She could have said, *And he knows more about eating disorders than you or Dad.* But she didn't get snippy and the sorrow on her face broke me yet again.

"I'm glad I'll be talking with Dr. Nathan soon," I said.

"Me too. You'll feel better then. I just wish you could have more fun when you visit me. All you do is get upset. Let's hike this afternoon. You're leaving tomorrow and we should enjoy today."

I couldn't imagine her hiking and burning calories so we settled on visiting the Clos du Bois winery near Sonoma. As we stood at the sampling bar, a wine expert educated us on the traces of pear and lemons, the citrus flavors in the white wine. She spoke of food pairings, what wine compliments fish and chicken and Rachel nodded as if this were her passion. Rachel, like many with anorexia, discussed food with gusto while taking meager bites. As the driver, she took only a few sips of wine. As the passenger, I tried all six wines plus the cheese and crackers. A lightweight drinker, I wobbled to the car and napped during the ride through the lush countryside.

On Monday I awoke at five to leave for the San Francisco International Airport. I'd kept the window open all night and by morning birdsong mixed with the crunch of gravel as commuters pulled out of their driveways. As difficult as the week had been, as much as I'd failed to get Rachel into more aggressive treatment, I'd miss her and these lovely fog-shrouded dawns. Thirty minutes before boarding my flight eastward I stopped at Starbucks. While drinking my coffee that felt like oxygen on a Mount Everest climb, Dr. Nathan called.

Public places, like jam-packed coffee shops, are tough spots for medical updates. You find yourself yelling into the phone, or saying, *Could you please repeat that, it's noisy here.* Despite the setting, Dr. Nathan offered all the time I needed. He understood how much Rachel resisted more intensive treatment, but he hoped that within a few weeks she'd change her mind. He'd been hearing from Abigail and Tom on a regular basis. He knew Rachel never missed her appointments and seemed willing to make positive changes, albeit small ones. The ongoing major problem remained her continual weight loss. Though he couldn't share her exact weight (the one detail Rachel didn't give HIPPA permission for), we both agreed on how bad she looked. Fortunately, her lab work and her vital signs remained stable, though he warned that this could change at any time. He said he'd do anything he could to expedite Rachel's admission to either a hospital or residential program once she agreed to go. Without either of these programs, he couldn't foresee recovery. His compassion and expertise restored me almost as much as overpriced coffee.

While walking to my gate I thought about the importance of lab work and vital signs in eating disorders. Rachel's weekly normal ones reassured her that "I can't be that bad if everything comes back okay." Yes, I'd tell her, they're fine now but they might not be tomorrow. These labs included a complete blood count to check for anemia, and a comprehensive metabolic profile to track electrolytes, glucose, and calcium as well as kidney and liver functions.

Of these, we were most concerned with an electrolyte imbalance, especially low potassium and magnesium that can alter normal heart rhythm. These imbalances cause prolonged QT intervals, which left untreated, can lead to a fatal ventricular fibrillation. Rachel understood this. One can rightfully ask, well if she did, why didn't she stop what she was doing? Believe me, if she could have, she would have.

Heart rate and blood pressure are seriously affected by weight loss. Patients below 80 percent of their normal weight experience bradycardia (a heart rate of less than 60 beats per minute) as well as hypotension, (a blood pressure less than 90/50). These readings should not be confused with a healthy athlete at peak cardiovascular training. However, for Rachel, like Mike, Mark, and me, we all have low heart rates and blood pressures to begin with.

Prior to weight loss, Rachel's resting heart rate was 50–60 beats per minute, and her blood pressure stayed close to 100/60; anorexia had dropped her heart rate to a consistent 39–40 beats per minute but so far, hadn't affected her blood pressure.

The body works damn hard to save itself when starved. The parasympathetic nervous system, part of the involuntary nervous system, attempts to slow the heart rate to conserve energy in the anorexic state. However, heart muscle is still weakened and simply can't pump blood as efficiently. This causes lowered blood pressure as well as orthostatic blood pressure changes (i.e., blood pressures that vary with lying, sitting, and standing). Often these varying blood pressures signal a need for hospitalization.

All this roiled around in my mind as I boarded the plane. Mark and I hoped my visit, and his phone calls and emails, might have convinced Rachel to enter treatment. Our utter failure to do so left us frustrated and frightened. Rachel's body had taken a beating and as I slid into my aisle and took the window seat, I also felt beat up and frazzled. A few minutes after hearing the ever-congenial instructions dealing with crashes on land and sea, I pressed my face against the window and wept. I'm not sure if the man beside me saw my quaking shoulders but if so, he ignored me. Feeling profoundly lost at thirty thousand feet above Earth, I wondered if heaven was close enough to hear me calling.

One afternoon two weeks later Rachel called. Panic filled her voice. "I'm in the ER," she said. "My heart started racing at school. Someone called 911."

I feared this would happen, this complication we had warned her about. My own heart skipped a few beats. "What's being done?" I asked in a surreal voice.

"I had an EKG and lab work. My potassium is a little low so I'll need to take a supplement. The ER doctor says I'm in normal sinus rhythm now; well, normal except for my low heart rate, but I can be discharged. He wants me to get a full cardiac work-up within the next few weeks."

"Of course. How are you feeling?"

"Horrible. You won't believe what one of the nurses said."

I heard her crying.

"He pulled a chair by my bed and said he wanted to talk. He wondered why I was doing this to myself, why I was doing this to my parents. He made me feel so guilty."

"This is not your fault! Forget him! I wish I could be there with you." How I wanted to smack the nurse. In my Catholic college, the wise Sisters of Mercy insisted there was no place in our nursing practice for patient judgment.

If we erred in this, we were in trouble. Never piss off a nun. However, this nurse was yet another example of how even well-meaning professionals can lack knowledge about eating disorders. I hoped the ER doc was better informed and after speaking with him, I felt satisfied with his competent care. As frightening as this episode was, he didn't feel Rachel needed hospital admission that day. I promised she'd have an immediate cardiac work-up. I spoke with Rachel again and said I'd fly to Santa Rosa soon.

"I'll do anything you ask," she said.

She knew she hovered over a cliff, and Mark and I thought, *Thank God, she's returned to her senses.*

A reflection from Rachel's journal:

> *On April 30, 2007, I believed all my fears were coming true. As I was teaching a lesson to the first graders on that hot afternoon, I felt an arrhythmia in my heart and I tried to breathe through it. My heart would not regulate. I truly thought I was going to die in front of the twenty beautiful angels I treasured so deeply. My life literally flashed before me and I saw my parents' horror as they heard the news. I felt desperately terrible for not agreeing to get help and I couldn't breathe. I thought I was going to pass out and once I got help in the room, I ran to a friend who knew the whole situation. I was rushed to the emergency room. I arrived at the hospital and, after all the tests were completed, I was later released. I knew at this time I had received another chance.*
>
> *I talked to my parents and agreed to begin inpatient treatment after the school year ended. This was a big step for me but looking back, this time though not too late was far later than ideal.*
>
> *May 1st was the first day I ever took off from AmeriCorps where my compulsive tendencies ruled every day, every moment, no matter the circumstances. No personal days even if they were needed. I could not miss a second of work or, in my mind, my world would have collapsed. Everyone at work supported me and they were all concerned but I refused to leave until school ended.*

Chapter Twelve

Vermont and California, 2007

After my shift ended the next Friday afternoon, I asked my head nurse, Terry, if we could talk. One of the best nurse leaders I've ever worked with, there isn't one aspect of running a large multispecialty clinic she doesn't understand. If ever any of us needed help she, like Clifford, saved the day. And she dealt with sick children, frightened children, and even a few bratty ones with a rare blend of humor and competence. Parents leaned on her confidence and knowledge; doctors relied on her decision-making and if some scientist could clone her, hospitals would benefit. Now, as she sat at my workstation desk, I warned her that I had bad news. I'd need more time off. Never the words a head nurse wants to hear when it's after five on Friday and there's yet another fire to douse.

"Rachel gets thinner by the week," I said. "I'll need to stay in California until we can get her into a residential program."

Terry looked at me and I thought she'd say no way, she's sorry but she's short staffed. If Rachel needs me that much, perhaps I should take a leave of absence or resign. For a second I forgot I was talking to Terry, the one who somehow pulled us through every small or large work crisis.

"You take as much time off as Rachel needs," she said. And then she spoke as if in a confessional. "I became bulimic at sixteen. I graduated at the top of my class, had college scholarships, showed horses for their owners, and it looked like I had everything going for me. But I didn't. This has been a hell of a day and when I get home tonight, there's a good chance I'll puke up dinner."

Her gaze deepened. "Fix Rachel now, while she still has a chance. I think I'm beyond that. Take all the time you need," she repeated. "We'll work something out here."

Terry's admission stunned me for I'd never guessed her history. Now I see Terry as the face of millions with eating disorders, of those who struggle daily with an illness controlling them, but due to their normal weights, their symptoms go unseen. "Thank you," I told her. "You have no idea how much you're helping me."

I think people say that to Terry every day.

But I couldn't return to Santa Rosa yet. Mark and I were needed in New Jersey. Fran had been hospitalized yet again for another plugged pancreatic duct stent. Fran had yet to agree on chemo, radiation, or surgery but month after month, she stayed alive despite having only basic treatment. We visited her in the hospital the day after I spoke with Terry. Fran looked too frail to even roll over in bed without help, but from her point of view, she had a brand new stent and wanted to hit the road. Again, Fran's resilience astounded me. Perhaps that's where Rachel's came from. I do know they shared that same stubborn streak when it came to the more aggressive treatment they both required. Fran loved talking with her friends about her son who was a doctor, but she had no interest whatsoever in listening to his or any other doctor's advice.

"Who needs it!" she said when Mark discussed surgery with her before we left the hospital that day. And so that conversation ended. We packed her bags and took off. Fran mustered enough energy that weekend to walk the boardwalk; and looking back, what a better view than watching chemo drip into your veins.

Two weeks later I returned to Santa Rosa. We all knew that the tightrope on which Rachel balanced had frayed months before and could snap any moment. She needed residential care immediately. The cutoff Body Mass Index (BMI) for residential programs is fifteen, but during the time she'd been selecting one, her BMI had lowered to 12.8. Only centers with partial or full hospitalization units would now accept her. After talking with admissions counselors and studying various programs, Rachel felt that the Center for Hope of the Sierras was the best fit for her.

I did too. The director and founder, Dr. Wendell, held dual certification in neurology and psychiatry. This extensive training allowed her to thoroughly understand and treat eating disorders from both a medical and a behavioral viewpoint. This resonated with all of us. We also liked the follow-up studies done on recovery rates of patients treated there. Yet beyond clinical expertise and success rates, we noted something else in our extended phone calls with her. An abiding respect for the patient. Dignity. Kindness. However, we'd lost several weeks dickering over treatment options. By the time Rachel had finally agreed to "go when the semester ended" she didn't qualify for admission.

Frantic phone calls ensued from Rachel and me to the Center's internist, Dr. Holt. Dr. Wendell and Dr. Holt would make an exception because Rachel's vital signs and labs remained stable. However, if she deteriorated or had changes in those labs and vital signs, she'd be transferred to a hospital for the placement of a feeding tube.

"I couldn't stand that," Rachel said as she finished her yogurt and berries on a Wednesday morning. "I eat three meals a day. I never skip a meal. I just need larger portions."

Those larger portions of scrambled eggs and turkey bacon stared her in the face. I asked her to eat half of them. She poked them with a fork, had a few bites, and then stopped.

"You might need a feeding tube," I said.

"No way. It will never come to that. And that's one of the reasons why I like the Center for Hope. They don't do feeding tubes."

I didn't like the schoolteacher's authority in her voice. "If you want to go there, you need to do it now," I said. "Not in another two weeks. I can tell you're weaker."

"Since Dr. Nathan asked me to work only a half-day, I'm feeling better. But I'm still waiting until the end of the school year. And some days I skip the gym."

Conversation over.

Another week passed and Rachel's twenty-third-birthday was coming up. Illness and stress don't justify skipping a celebration. During these times, friends and music, cake and flowers sustain us. They give the party an even richer meaning for not just the occasion but for life itself. At dawn on Rachel's birthday the sparrows woke me up. Maybe, I hoped, they were good omens.

Rachel had already left for the gym. I couldn't watch her self-destruction by elliptical so I stayed home and took an early morning walk through her neighborhood. Walking had long been my way to make sense out of the world. I started this young, around age four. On occasion my slightly older cousin and I had been found traipsing far from our backyards. We could disappear faster than a magician's bunny. I suppose some would call this running away, but to me and Linda, we were exploring. We meant no harm. Early childhood memory is full of lacunae so one never knows what actually happened from what is *remembered* as happening.

Were Linda and I punished for wandering? My memory says no. Were deals cut? Bribes offered? That's more likely. I do know we stopped taking off for at least several more years. And if I behaved like the good girl my mother tried to make me, my father would walk with me after work. He preferred a few blocks, I begged for more, and in those spaces around the vacant areas of memory, I saw us hand-in-hand as days settled into nights. A generation later I'd see his fierce handgrip on Mike and Rachel as they walked together. No doubt he thought they'd be like me. Fleet and ready to run.

Rachel's neighborhood provided excellent walking. On her birthday morning I passed Spanish-style homes with bougainvillea trailing from porch railings before turning onto a worn trail between cul-de-sacs to a still undeveloped old ranch land. Ten acres of dirt, dust, and bleached overgrown grass centered me more than any suburban sidewalk. I tried to imagine what old Santa Rosa looked like back in its cattle days and wished more of it had survived.

I had a busy day ahead. First, I'd clean the house. I'd already asked the three housemates if they'd minded me doing so. Not to worry, they were quite pleased. I called my housekeeping partial rent and this satisfied all of us. I didn't explain that washing floors, cleaning bathrooms, vacuuming rugs, scouring grunge from stovetops, and polishing granite counters happened to be my marijuana, which I had noted, but not mentioned, in abundance there.

By midmorning the house looked like it belonged to tidy law-abiding folks so I decided to walk a mile to the local supermarket. Unlike the Whole Foods where Rachel shopped, this one was affordable. There were no artful displays of pricey prepared foods that appeared Photoshopped. No twenty-foot salad bars filled with the best produce grown in Sonoma Valley. Here, shoppers used food stamps. Here, people looked chiseled by time and circumstance and I fit right in. Amidst the ordinariness of this tired, outdated store, a lineup of turquoise, orange, yellow, and lime green animal piñatas dangled from a wire far above the meat counters. Piñata heaven! A clerk cut my choice, a big blue donkey, from the herd and I added this prize to my cart. Then I bought a chocolate cake that all of us except Rachel would eat. I knew that she'd at least be happy blowing out the candles and I wondered what she'd wish for.

The trip home took fine balancing skills for I'd overstuffed my backpack with food and drinks, I carried a string-tied bakery box, and an iridescent piñata rode on my shoulder. At times I saw people giving me strange looks. I'm not sure if this was because I was a white lady in a Latine neighborhood or if it was because I was a loco white lady wearing a paper donkey.

While walking, I thought about the importance of celebrations for sick children and their families. In a life ruled by a grim diagnosis or a severe injury, in a life interrupted by tests and treatments, the party says you can still have fun. Be almost normal. You still get to blow out the candles. As important as this is for the child, it's even more so for the parents. For a few blessed hours the anxiety switch is turned off. As I lugged my load home, I felt more relaxed than I had in weeks.

Rachel awaited me at the house. She stood by the couch, jiggling the car keys in her hands. "I have a thirty-minute break and came to pick you up for school," she said in a stern schoolteacher voice. She didn't like me walking in a rough neighborhood. I reminded her that it was daytime and chances are, I'd be safe.

"I don't want you shopping alone in Santa Rosa ever again!" And then her teacher's voice sweetened. "Do you have any idea how much I worry about you? I can't have anything happen to you. I'm telling you right now that when you're an old lady I'm leashing you to keep you safe."

I hoped she'd live long enough to do so. I recalled Olivia, Mike's Kiwi friend, who had spent her twenty-third birthday with us. Now I worried that my wishes and prayers would ring hollow because faith seemed as fragile as the pink petals on Olivia's birthday lilies.

Rachel's birthday party took off in fine form. Her housemates and her AmeriCorps friends, a tight group, came and we shared pizza, fruit platters, grilled chicken, chips, salsa, and guacamole. We drank beer and wine and when it was time for candles, Rachel blew out every one. Another good omen. I smiled as the smoke from each candle wafted upward.

Our donkey friend hanging from the garage rafter proved nearly indestructible. One blindfolded guest after another whacked away at the tough cardboard body without success. In the second round, the donkey finally cracked and spewed out Hershey chocolates, packs of chewing gum, peanut butter cups, and cheap bracelets. These ten young adults were just as enthusiastic as the younger ones I remembered years ago at our kids' birthday parties. After claiming the loot, the kids turned down the garage lights and turned up the music. We were ready to dance.

Poet and dance critic Edwin Denby wrote that there is a bit of insanity in dancing that does everyone a great deal of good. Yes. How right he was. When standing at a street corner you should act normal. You shouldn't contort your body, do a bump and a grind, throw your arms skyward, or sing out loud. If you did, people might think you unhinged or even dangerous. But if you add music, the darkened floor of a ballroom, a smoky bar, or even a dim two-car garage, you suddenly begin to feel better. The pulsating rhythms free your chained feet and the lyrics that fill your mind push sadder words away.

The nuns at my Catholic college knew this. Therefore, every so often they coerced us into spending an evening at the state psychiatric hospital so we could dance with the patients. Many of these patients lived in locked wards, patients shut off from the world, patients who shuffled and drooled due to psychotropic drugs, but when they danced, oh when they danced, they came alive. I recall one man pulling me close, his face wet on my shoulder, and saying how girls felt "just like foam rubber." I'd heard plenty worse from sane men so I happily finished our dance.

And I was happy dancing with my daughter. A tyrannical anorexia dictated our days and for the most part, happiness lingered in the distant past. But for an hour I ignored anorexia. Rachel and I did our bump and grind, the kind we'd done dozens of times in the kitchen while making dinner and dancing, but here Rachel's hip was a knife cutting into me. I didn't feel the pain. Neither did she. This is what dancing does for our souls. It's such a potent human connection that even the Sisters of Mercy swear by it.

Later we sat around the candlelit living room. We drank more wine and beer and the music played low. Either from fatigue or booze, the guests grew melancholy. Most of them spoke about tough times. Broken love affairs. Broken homes, troubles with drugs or alcohol. One spoke about coming out to her family.

"Well," Rachel said from her corner of the sofa. "It's obvious how I ruined my life. I had a bone density test. I've got the bones of an old lady. So I may as well tell you now. I'm finally going to the treatment center for eating disorders. It's the only way I'll get better. I'm leaving in a few days and ending my contract a week early."

"You're really doing this?" her friend Ava asked. She'd been primed for an intervention like the ones we'd been covertly watching on cable TV.

"Yeah, I promise you guys won't have to drag me into the car."

Ava smiled. "We'll all be here when you leave. Just in case you change your mind."

That night, filled with pizza, watermelon, gooey chocolate cake, and hope, I slept four straight hours. The next morning I felt as mellow as after yoga class. Rachel seemed peaceful too and on that Saturday we chatted comfortably over our scrambled eggs, yogurt, and sliced strawberries.

"My friends are amazing," she said as we basked in the warmth of the gas fireplace. "Aren't they fun?"

"I'll say. I appreciated their offers to be here when we leave for the Center for Hope. And I especially liked their offer to help in case you won't get into the car."

Rachel sipped her coffee and then looked me straight in the eye. I didn't like that look. "We need to talk," she said matter-of-factly. "Now that school is almost out, I'll have more time to focus on my health. I've decided to stay right here and continue my outpatient program."

I went numb and speechless. Couldn't even drink my coffee. I knew her outpatient program had no clout with her illness. When her therapist said any day she'd turn things around, I'd think any day, she'll have cardiovascular collapse. Asystole.

"And Mom, here's the best idea yet. You could take a leave of absence. You need a long vacation and you could stay here with me and cook."

Still silent, I scooped eggs onto my trembling fork. Dazed, almost knocked out, I noted Rachel's good mood. She even ate her eggs with gusto.

"Rachel," I croaked. "I already do all the cooking when I'm here. And most of the eating. Another month wouldn't accomplish anything except more weight loss."

"This is my decision and I am an adult. I think I know what's best for me. Honestly, I'm opposed to how much those residential programs charge. We'd be broke in no time. Besides, I'm getting great therapy right here."

I didn't agree but arguing would have proved worthless.

"You know," she said, "we've heard that women in treatment centers learn bad habits from one another. It's possible that I could get more entrenched in an eating disorder there."

I couldn't imagine her more entrenched. I knew if I stayed in the kitchen I'd soon regret my words. I took a deep yoga breath and then a few more. "Let's go for a walk. It's a gorgeous morning. We can talk outside."

"I'd like that." She spoke agreeably but I wasn't in agreement mode.

We walked down her winding street, past the pink and beige adobe homes with their overflowing bougainvillea, and then I nudged Rachel between the cul-de-sacs and onto the worn path leading to the vacant ranchland. The place where I could think. As we walked, a cacophony of her excuses looped in my memory.

I can't cook in my kitchen. Mice everywhere! Look at all the healthy fruits and veggies I'm eating. I know you think I'm thin, but I look just like my dad. I can't eat more right now because I probably have irritable bowel syndrome. I'm lactose intolerant so I can't drink those shakes you gave me. Bread bloats me. I'm fine! I feel so good after working out for two hours. I'm fine. I am fine! And finally, *I've decided not to go to a residential program after all. Just give me another month.*

My head throbbed from those words and from all the times I'd heard them and then watched, waited, hoped. I knew this day wasn't only about Rachel's intervention. It was about mine. Today I'd reclaim my disappearing daughter and say damn it, *you will live.*

As we walked, lambent sunshine danced across a cluster of orchid shooting stars swaying in the tall grass. A choir of robins sang out. Inspired by this crystalline day, and by my own determination, I'd no longer bow before anorexia. No one, especially Rachel, would prevent me from getting her the help she desperately needed.

"I need to tell you something," I said with rock-hard intent. "You've deteriorated. You know that. You're exhausted and weak. And sometimes dizzy."

Rachel nodded.

"I'm not wasting time today. No small talk. You have three options. You can enter a residential program like the Center for Hope tomorrow. Not in a week, or a month. Or you can be admitted to either Cornell or Stanford's In-patient Eating Disorders Program. You can also choose not to do any of these. But, if so, I'm calling my lawyer and he will contact a judge for a court order to have you immediately committed to a psychiatric unit." Those words burned my throat like acid.

Rachel looked stricken, as if I'd knocked the wind out of her. "You wouldn't!" she cried.

I tapped my jeans pocket, the one holding my cell phone. "I have my lawyer on speed dial and I'll call him in a second."

What we believe is often more compelling than what we can prove. Rachel believed I'd do this and that was a good thing. I hadn't talked to my lawyer in ten years and furthermore, I still didn't know how to speed dial.

"Fine! I'll go to the Center for Hope," she spit back at me.

"We leave at six a.m. on Sunday."

"No way, Mom. I'm not leaving before ten. And I'll drive."

"A deal." My voice softened. "But remember this. Someday your dad and I will be old farts. If we're dangerous drivers, you can take our keys. And if we're not safe living alone, you can send us to a nursing home. You'll be in charge of us when we aren't safe. But now, you aren't safe."

She knew that.

We smiled wanly, circled our arms around each other, and cried. Our tears were brief because we had a car to pack and a future to build. The song of the thrushes rang out, the upward lilt of their melodic phrases my talisman for a new day.

Chapter Thirteen

California and Nevada, 2007

Rachel sticks by her words and doesn't leave much wiggle room for the change of mind or heart. Though I had us packed and ready to peel out of town by nine on Sunday, she wouldn't budge until ten. Five friends escorted us to the car and they'd have hog-tied her into the backseat if she'd balked. Those friends had been rock solid, and of that group, Joy had been stellar. We were indebted to all of them. "We made you a birthday and farewell gift," one said as she handed Rachel a hand-stitched blanket. "Something to remember us by."

"Thank you so much," Rachel said to the group. Graciousness kicked in. No over-the-top TV drama. "I'll miss you guys."

We had a long hugging session and then Rachel asked for my car keys. "I'd like to drive," she said in the teacher's voice. "You ride shotgun."

I took my seat, fished my prescription sunglasses from my pocketbook, and noticed my right lens was missing. Not the first time. I searched through my bag without luck and thought that once I attended to the disarray within it, I'd find the lens. I put on my regular sunglasses and off we went.

Every good road trip has a song that will be forever linked to a certain stretch of open highway covered at a certain point in life. Rachel and I channeled Amy Winehouse, because her "Rehab" became that song for us on the way to Nevada. Like Amy, Rachel had said *no* to rehab and Mark and I'd said *yes, yes, yes*. I imagined Amy's parents wanted her back in treatment after the Internet showed her looking rail thin and strung out. I knew exactly how her parents worried that their gifted twenty-three-year-old Jewish daughter would self-destruct.

I heard Amy's protesting wail as we headed southeast. Rachel joined in on the refrain in a voice buckling with anger. Maybe that same anger would spur her on to fight anorexia.

I had my own anger. Not with her, just with her illness. And with Mark and I for all that we'd done wrong, for his obsessive running, his war on cholesterol, his attitude about my weight and of course, I was angry with myself. The first time Mark ever complained about my weight I should have tossed the menorah at him and yelled, *Don't you dare speak to me this way again.* Instead I slipped into complacency and sometimes even apologized about not being my former skinny bride self. And when Fran grilled me about my weight, when she'd say, *Oh, you gained a few,* I should have spoken up. After all, she was the one being rude, not me. But in my self-imposed role as family peacemaker I'd forged peace at too high a price. I'd swallowed my words instead of using them rightfully.

And I was pissed that I allowed myself to feel less worthy as a not-so-skinny woman, that I'd bought diet books and tried to taper my appetite even though I never succeeded beyond a week. However, the message I'd sent Rachel came out loud and clear. If the woman she respected the most waffled with diets and sucked up criticism from her husband, weight mattered.

You bet I yelled, "No," along with Amy Whitehouse.

Halfway to Reno, we stopped at a Whole Foods in a Sacramento suburb. This pleased Rachel as Whole Foods served her kinds of meals: organic greens and grilled chicken. I craved pork barbecue but not finding any, had salad and chicken as well. Two hours down, two more to go before Reno. So far, Rachel's driving had been tolerable. How hard she must have been working on that.

The mountain pass into Nevada swept through heavily forested steep mountains. Being in these mountains felt like home and safety. And I believed Rachel would soon be safer at the Center for Hope than in Santa Rosa. In addition to the psychiatric and nutritional support, she'd be seeing Dr. Holt several times per week. Her labs would be carefully monitored, the nursing staff would check her vital signs twice daily, and if her condition changed, she'd enter a hospital program. For the first time in months I felt like we were well positioned for recovery. Maybe the heavy dread I carried would lighten.

Illness, I'd often discuss with parents, is not always about being on high alarm every moment. It's about finding whatever pleasure you can in the day, about laughing over inane things, and even permitting self-care. It's the opposite of martyrdom, living for the right cause instead of dying for it. In need of serious self-care, I loosened my tense gunshot posture and slept as Rachel drove through the evergreens.

I woke up an hour later.

"Good nap?" Rachel asked.

"Yes."

"I'm glad. You needed it."

"I'm getting excited about seeing the Center for Hope. I've looked at the website so often that I can close my eyes and still see it." I imagined the lush, well-irrigated lawn, the white porch swings, and the peaceful koi pond.

"I'm excited too," she said. "I can't wait to go hiking around Lake Tahoe. And I'd really like to be in a consistent yoga program. The website didn't show a gym and that concerns me."

"We'll see," I answered, invoking the quintessential parent escape line.

In midafternoon we pulled into the front parking lot of the Center for Hope. The large white contemporary cape-style house, Rachel's new digs, looked well-maintained and inviting. A rustic split-rail fence bordered the far side of the property, and a profusion of pink roses bloomed along its length. Other neighbors had extensive rose gardens as well. This was Reno? I'd expected only sunburned lawns and stretches of casinos. The roses were another good omen. We got out of the car and exchanged those oh-my-God-what's-next looks.

A forty-something woman with a welcoming smile strode up to us. "I'm Penny," she said. "One of the residential advisors." Penny shook our hands firmly as she welcomed us.

"Let me help you with your luggage." She looked dismayed by how much we'd crammed into the CRV. "People don't usually bring this much," she told us.

We explained that Rachel had moved out of her house and everything she owned came with her. What she couldn't keep inside she'd lock up in her Honda. Or she'd mail some of the boxes home. For now, we'd just take in the suitcases.

"I'll carry them," the RA offered.

I could read the RA's thoughts. How could someone Rachel's size lift anything? I reached into the trunk for the big suitcase so full that I'd sat on it so I could zip it up.

"Oh, you shouldn't do that," the RA cautioned. "You could hurt your back."

Ever polite, I didn't laugh or even grin. We certainly didn't have a bellboy when we'd packed earlier in the morning and by the time Rachel's friends arrived, we'd filled the car without fuss or herniated discs.

The RA struggled to pick up the suitcases but couldn't. "I'm getting some help," she told us. "There's no way I can do this alone."

Apparently, the Nevada woman was a city girl who didn't haul water buckets, carry hay bales, or push wheelbarrows brimming with wet manure across a rainy, deeply rutted pasture. While she sought reinforcements, I pulled out the larger suitcase, Rachel the smaller, and we walked through the front door. My heart pounded but not from exertion.

Now two RAs were ready to help but we gripped our suitcases hard, as if relinquishing them meant handing over a piece of us. The RAs led us through a sunny living room with a massive stone fireplace and we followed them into an adjacent bedroom. The young woman standing inside, Rachel's new roommate, had a big smile and immense eyes. Tall like Rachel, slender but not alarmingly so, the girls could have been cousins. We made our introductions and I asked Ella how she got to the Center for Hope. I meant did she drive or fly, but she interpreted my question as asking what brought her. In a rush she explained that her older sister, a doctor, discovered her bulimia and said, *You're getting on a plane and spending the summer in treatment.* Ella had arrived the night before and looked as relieved to see Rachel as Rachel did meeting her. I sensed these girls would become great friends.

A few minutes later the RA interrupted our conversation, as she needed to inspect Rachel's clothes, makeup, and personal items. "Where are your drugs?" she asked in an even-keeled nonjudgmental way. Rachel handed her a jar of gummy bear vitamins, a packet of birth control pills, and a small bottle of Advil. The woman looked disgruntled and told Rachel that she needed to see *all* her drugs.

"That's it." Rachel told her.

"Drugs aren't her problem," I said. "Not eating much is the problem."

The efficient RA then searched for sharps. Had Rachel hid paper clips, razor blades, or knives in her panties or T-shirts? Relentlessly she searched for small weapons of destruction.

Rachel explained that she didn't cut and the RA looked to me for verification.

"She's never cut," I told her.

"Are you certain?" the woman asked and Rachel nodded yes. Continuing her search, the RA ran her fingers under the edges of Rachel's hair straightening iron, feeling for any contraband. Not finding any, she peered at Rachel's stringy arms for linear white scars. I appreciated her thoroughness in this introductory safety check.

Upon conclusion of her check, the RA asked me to wait in the great room, as one of the staff would interview Rachel in private. I left and sunk into a beige corduroy couch flanking the fireplace. Young women passed in and out of the room and smiled at me. I watched them and thought, *Gee, you don't look emaciated at all.*

A blonde woman of a most normal weight sat next to me in a matching corduroy chair. She put her book down, and told me her name was Madison. I liked the honeyed tone in her voice as she reassured me that Rachel had found an excellent treatment center, one where people recovered. "I'm a psychiatrist," she said. "I became anorexic in college and stayed that way through medical school and residency. I've been here six months. The Center for Hope is amazing. I'm better and your daughter will be too."

Madison glowed. Clear mountain air, sunshine, and the best of therapy had worked for her. As Madison and I were talking about our New England roots, another woman approached with a smile and an outstretched hand.

"Rachel," she said loudly. "Welcome to the Center for Hope. We're so glad that you've come here."

I wondered what about me looked like an anorexic woman. It took a few seconds to remind myself that we tend to stereotype those with anorexia. We think of the perfectionistic white female adolescent with a dance or gymnastic background. We don't often consider race, gender, or age diversity. But already at the Center for Hope I'd seen an Asian girl, a Black girl, and a middle-aged woman.

"I'm Nancy, Rachel's mother," I said.

"And I'm Meredith. An RA. How are you doing?"

Had my deep-breathing, relaxed posture really looked like someone hyperventilating and too weary to sit tall? Before anorexia I maintained privacy. If someone had asked me that question, I'd simply have answered, *Fine, and how are you?* However, my filters had dropped. Just like Ella, I gushed out our story like a broken fire hydrant spewing water.

I talked about Australia. Rachel's time in AmeriCorps, the failed outpatient program, the many deaths affecting Rachel, and then ended with her resistance to a residential program. In addition to blurting this all out, I added details about Rachel's weight in Australia, her weight back in Vermont, and then faithfully chronicled her weight losses in Santa Rosa.

I noticed that the residents kept pacing back and forth across the great room to the kitchen. The aroma of freshly baked cookies drew me in, so I guessed it did the same to them. Meredith, the RA, looked worried, maybe horrified. Finally, she leaned into me and whispered, "We don't talk weight here," she said with the precision of one detonating a bomb. "That's considered triggering behavior."

Knowing that I'd triggered everyone made me so nervous that I needed to pee. I apologized for my ignorance and asked to use the ladies room. Meredith offered to take me there. Odd, I thought, but perhaps Nevada cordiality. We entered the hall opposite Rachel's new room and Meredith unlocked the bathroom door. "I'm sorry," she said. "We monitor our guests as well as our residents."

I don't pee well with listeners so I ran the faucet full force. I imagined how Rachel would accept bathroom patrol and I guessed it wouldn't be appreciated. Only a few days before she had patrolled first graders intent on bathroom mayhem if left alone for too long. I visualized her jogging double time while washing her hands, or worse, feigning constipation and fitting in several sets of abdominal crunches while calling, *I'll be out in a minute.*

I assumed that at the Center for Hope, Rachel would quickly develop a tiny bladder. Part of me resented how her privacy would be invaded, her sense of dignity abolished. The wiser part of me said that left to her dignity, Rachel would add several mini workouts to her treatment plans. Yes, the bathroom cop should be there.

After the triggering fiasco, Meredith directed me to Dr. Holt's office located on the far side of the fragrant-smelling kitchen. Dr. Holt, our benefactress, had been the one saying, *I know Rachel's weight is far below our guidelines but she's medically stable. Let's give her a chance.* Without her intervention, Rachel would be in a hospital bed.

Dr. Holt exuded the warmth of a midwestern cook inviting you into her cozy kitchen for roast beef and mashed potatoes. "So glad to see you made it here," she said as she stood and shook my hand. "I knew Rachel hesitated about coming and I feared she might back out at the last minute."

"She tried to. But I threatened her with a court order. She didn't like that idea much."

"I expect not. Have a seat. I'd like to go over some family history with you. This is important information in understanding and treating eating disorders."

Did we have any family members with eating disorders? I told her there was no one we knew about, though Mark had strong beliefs about food and exercise and his mother described people by their size and weight. At that point I hadn't made the connections about "strong beliefs" and "describing people by their size and weight" with any pathology.

And what about my side of the family, Dr. Holt asked.

Both sides of my family rarely missed a good meal, I laughed, or a snack at any time of day. Or in the middle of the night. With age most of us had gained weight; some worried about this, others didn't.

Dr. Holt then wondered about a history of anxiety in our families.

History? I grinned at that one. We all came newly minted straight out of the hatch with anxiety. Some had anxiety complicated with obsessive-compulsive symptoms. My mother and Mark's mother shared the high-strung temperaments of racehorses and in the era before women understood wellness, their respective doctors kept them mildly sedated and socially acceptable for three decades.

"Plenty of anxiety," I told her.

I explained that fortunately we didn't have much depression on either side; chances are we wore ourselves out with worry instead. Lately though, I'd seen Rachel's mood decline. Anorexia had made her sad. Notice: I hadn't recognized yet that it was the other way around.

Dr. Holt suspected that Rachel was indeed depressed and she'd be evaluated for this. "Anorexia," she said, "rarely exists as a primary disorder."

I nodded. I'd been as blinded by Rachel's pretense of happiness as I'd been by her anorexia, but now I was distinguishing new steps in our family dance: Rachel practiced good will in the family dynamic like I practiced peace. But we'd suffered small and large fractures along the way.

The family history quest continued. Did we have a history of alcohol or drug addiction?

In my Irish family where liquor ebbed and flowed like tides? I mentioned my uncle and the events preceding his stretch at Attica. I mentioned my great-aunt fingering her rosary bead and her flask, and hardest for me, my mother taking prescription drugs. I said I'd shied away from drugs and alcohol since I'd been a teenager because I feared I'd be sucked under fast.

Did Rachel drink or use drugs? In high school, I said, Rachel abstained out of both fear and obedience. She'd studied compulsively freshman year in college and didn't party often. Parties escalated sophomore year and she had a stint of binge drinking, soon cured by one night of hourly vomiting. As for drugs, she'd occasionally smoke a joint.

Before ending our interview, Dr. Holt asked about the heights and weights in our immediate family. After hearing these numbers, she felt that Mike and Rachel were genetically predisposed to being lean and having fast metabolisms. I agreed.

"Now what would your husband say about my weight?" she asked. "I'm guessing he'd call me overweight. But I look like those in *my* family. I have normal cholesterol levels, low blood pressure, and am healthy."

I didn't answer.

"You don't have to say anything. I get tired of all those doctors who think health is measured by a certain weight."

We then discussed Rachel's medical treatment as well as the close observation she'd have. For me, the Center for Hope had already worked. In this comfortable home bordered by roses, she'd have the clinical observation received in a hospital.

The final step in the afternoon included meeting one of the admissions staff along with Rachel to sign multiple legal documents regarding financial responsibility. Rachel, who prided herself on financial independence, flinched when I handed over a ten thousand dollar check as a deposit for her care.

She had her own documents to sign. The first, a list of regulations, presented no problem. She liked rules, and a classroom full of engaged, often loudly enthusiastic but still obedient kids pleased her. The admissions counselor read one particular rule out loud: "You must sign that you will eat 100 percent of the food served to you. We will consider the portion sizes carefully, but you must eat all meals and snacks."

Rachel checked that box with a flourish. "I'm here to get well," she said. "I'll do what I have to." Her voice rang out as confident, a voice ironically coupled with her physical fragility.

In my addled brain, foggy from insomnia yet buzzed from caffeine, I envisioned Rachel eating all her portions, not exercising, and gaining perhaps three pounds a week. Twelve pounds the first month, the second month, the third, and finally in the fourth month, the last six or seven pounds. I saw her cured and the nightmares over. Such optimism.

After signing that paperwork, the admissions counselor politely reminded me that I needed to say goodbye to Rachel but I could return for one hour in the morning before my flight home.

Rachel and I spoke briefly. I'd convinced myself that she felt as committed to recovery as I did. After all, her voice didn't falter as she signed her agreements. In my optimism sorely in need of a reality tune-up, I thought how lucky we were that Rachel was already adapting to her new life.

After we shared a lingering hug, Rachel and her roommate Ella settled on the back porch. Bottles of bright red nail polish were neither drugs nor cutting tools and as long as they painted their nails and didn't drink the nail polish remover, they could do manicures and pedicures.

I waved to them as I got behind the wheel of the Honda CRV but the right lens for my driving glasses remained unaccounted for. Due to my impaired vision, fatigue, and overall lack of direction, it took me only three blocks to lose myself in Reno. Frustrated with my ineptness, I pulled into a restaurant parking lot.

In dire need of the best comfort food around, I ordered a thick hamburger grilled medium, the staple of my childhood, and this one tasted like the ones my mother and I used to have at the Burger King back in Ithaca. Over the years I'd become a decent cook, and eaten at many fine restaurants, but stress me enough and I resort to summer days with my mom and a couple burgers. Long dead, she still kept me company.

The waitress provided me with directions that penetrated my brain fog. She even suggested what motels in Reno were safe. "Be careful," she warned. "Being a woman alone in Reno can be risky." I nodded, but where isn't it risky for a woman traveling alone?

After dinner I found my way to the Sands Hotel. I checked in, unpacked, and spent a few hours in the casino. I played a twenty-dollar bill and lost and regained it several times. It was close to midnight Vermont time when I returned to the room and called Mark. I knew he'd be awake because we'd never acquired the smart habit of early bedtimes.

"What a good day," I told him. "We had an easy four-hour drive from

Santa Rosa. The Center for Hope is homey, not institutional, and the staff seem professional yet warm. I like it here."

"How's Rachel?"

"Just amazing. She's strong and gracious. You'd be proud of her. It's as if she has finally decided to overcome this thing."

"I hope so."

Like me, Mark didn't begrudge Rachel. He no more blamed her for being anorexic than he did his mother for having cancer. But he did want the two of them being more proactive in their respective illnesses. "And how are you doing?" he asked. "Your voice is hoarse. Has your asthma kicked in?"

Mark once worried about Sudden Infant Death Syndrome. Now he worried about my breathing. Did I have my inhaler? Did I play the poker machines in the non-smoking rows of the casino? Did my room smell like cigarettes? Once I gave the right answers, I waited for the final question. Had I looked under the mattress corners for bed bugs? Bedbugs didn't have a prayer with that man. Not yet, I told him, but I will. I didn't say that my most pressing problem happened to be a missing lens and I was driving around Reno with one eye closed. Now that would have thrown him for sure.

We said we missed each other and whispered good night.

A stale smoke odor permeated the room but I lacked the energy to voice a complaint and maybe get a room upgrade. Instead I closed the crimson drapes and blocked the 24/7 flashing neon on the casino strip. In this darkened room, my bug-free bed felt comfortable, though undoubtedly well used. I ignored the saggy spots and slept quite well by my standards, one straight five-hour stretch.

After enjoying a full buffet breakfast I drove back to the Center for Hope. I only got lost once, a great success. Rachel met me at the door and I'd rarely seen her angrier.

"You won't believe this place," she said bitterly. "I have a horrible migraine. Every fifteen minutes someone shined a flashlight in my eyes. I'm exhausted. Oh, and they lock the bathroom door. Whenever I go to the bathroom I have to ask permission like a first grader. And someone listens in. I told *everyone* I wasn't bulimic but these are the rules. Oh, and they're starving me here. They didn't believe me when I said how much I'd been eating so they're giving me less than what I'm used to. They say I'll get sick if I eat too much."

"Okay, slow down, let's talk this through."

"Nothing to talk about. In thirty days I can sign myself out and that's exactly what I'm doing. No one can stop me then."

The past months collapsed around her like her thinned-out vertebrae could potentially do. She'd crashed into physical and emotional pieces; all bones, no flesh, despising the present, and planning an untenable escape. Leaving her now felt like abandonment.

"Let's go to the porch, honey. We can't debate this in the hallway."

Nevada morning sun bore down hot and clean after the smoky casino. Like me, Rachel craved sunlight, a side effect from living in cloudy Vermont. I thought that basking on the swings might lighten her mood. We rocked side by side on a white wood-slatted glider but the sun didn't do a damn thing for either of us. However, Rachel directed her galvanic anger at the Center for Hope and not at me. Though Mark and I had sent her here, we'd escaped her vitriol.

"I'm sorry you had such a bad night," I said. "Of course you'd feel terrible today."

"Well, just prepare yourself that I'm out of here in a month."

"Being here will keep you safe. You can't lose any more weight."

On one level, the rational one, Rachel heard me and agreed, but on the subterranean level I couldn't fathom, the voice of terrible discipline lashed out at her. All I could do was put my arms around her as we cried in utter frustration and sadness. After the sun had dried our faces dry, we returned to the air-conditioned living room. Here we'd say goodbye. We wedged together on the couch until she began shivering and went to her room for the green blanket her AmeriCorps friends had made. To my shock, Rachel cuddled on my lap and draped the blanket over us, like her younger self had done. I imagined how we looked: enmeshed mother and daughter, regressive behavior in the daughter, enabling behavior from the mother. I supposed an RA had jotted these observations in a journal for a therapist to deal with. Well, too damn bad. If this gave Rachel one moment of security, that's all I cared about. She felt like feathers on my lap and I could have held her for hours. She might have blown away but we stayed fast.

After five minutes Rachel regained her years and with composure, walked me to the door. We hugged, my muscle upon her bone, and I left her behind.

Rachel's eating disorder voice: *What a rip-off this place is. Notice your great welcoming meal. One large turkey meatball. You have a horrible migraine from no sleep because some RA shined a flashlight on your face every fifteen minutes. And this crap about eating 100% of your food is pure bullshit. IF you are ever given anything decent to eat, know this: You will not let yourself go, you will not get big as a pig. There's nothing wrong with you. Stay strong. Don't give in to anyone. And get your ass out of there in thirty days.*

Chapter Fourteen

Vermont, 2007

Move easily without consideration. This is what those of us lucky enough not to have the neurological disorders I saw at work can do. Long ago, nursing had humbled me, made me grateful for my own healthy body with muscles and nerves able to respond at a moment's notice. Mark, Mike, Rachel, and I had been blessed with the complex, elegant, and wondrous ability to move. Whenever and wherever, to move as easily as to breathe. We don't think about this life of easy movement until it's lost. Rachel forfeited movement at the Center for Hope and this delivered yet another blow to her identity.

On admission, Rachel had signed a statement agreeing to eat one hundred percent of her meals and snacks. Like signing a home mortgage, the real work of her owning her health became a constant and binding contract, one that if broken, had consequences.

At the core of Rachel's treatment lay the basic premise that movement was tied to food intake, and at a cellular level, to metabolism. During Rachel's outpatient treatment she'd been allowed to work out for those forty-five minutes I'd considered dangerous. She could use the elliptical, run on the treadmill, lift weights, practice yoga, or hike. Her therapists felt some exercise helped her mood as well as her bone density. I understood, but weighed her caloric expenditure, perhaps four hundred fifty calories depending on her workout, against her intake. During those last few weeks in Santa Rosa, that intake might have plummeted to five or six hundred calories daily. Exercise in addition to the constant motion of teaching only yielded more weight loss.

As with much in life, what is not said, what remains on the white spaces of a page, is also coded with information. We'd studied the Center for Hope website and noticed women hiking through the pine-covered mountains near Lake Tahoe, riding horseback along gentle trails in the foothills, or practicing yoga on-site. Rachel assumed that she'd be starting these activities immediately. We didn't know that those white spaces contained a different story; such activities were earned privileges after a certain level of restoration had occurred.

In walked Rachel's nutritionist, Dr. Leah Bell, aka Leah, to explain this. Rachel had a few years' experience with eating disorders; Leah had twenty-five years treating them. And her academic credentials were as honed as her experience.

Like Rachel, Leah had grown up in a small town in Vermont. Born with empathy hardwired by an all-around crap detector, Leah became Rachel's fierce match. Lean, fresh-faced, with well-behaved short hair and a military bearing, one almost felt the need to salute her when she entered a room.

"Leah is tough," Rachel said after their first meeting. "She's the law here. But the good part is how everyone loves her. She knows what she's talking about. And you know how much she cares by how hard she works for you."

Leah told Rachel right off that there wouldn't be any exercise. She'd preserve every calorie she took in. She couldn't even go upstairs to the second floor. Her one activity would be attending therapy sessions. Three times weekly she'd meet with Julie, her primary therapist. Once a week she'd meet with Dr. Wendell for a psychiatry session and twice weekly she'd meet with Leah. Two or three times daily she'd attend group therapy sessions.

In addition, every bite of food would be monitored, every bathroom trip escorted. Treatment would occur through the day and evening and during any brief remaining free time, she'd be on one of those comfortable corduroy couches in the great room or those wide porch swings. Getting well, she learned, would be her new career and the paycheck would be privileges. As she restored (the words *gaining weight* were off-limits), she'd be incrementally allowed more movement.

Leah calculated every meal and snack with the utmost precision to avoid a dangerous refeeding syndrome. Rachel's metabolism had been utilizing fat and protein to provide the energy that she'd normally derive from carbohydrates. Once carbohydrates were reintroduced, she could potentially experience an insulin shift as she resumed more carbohydrate usage. This insulin shift could result in abnormally low blood phosphate levels, and in turn, among other serious complications, lead rapidly to respiratory failure, hypotension, cardiac failure, and death. A fatal refeeding syndrome is not a rare occurrence.

This explained the lone turkey meatball for dinner the day Rachel had arrived. Until more lab work, as well as a thorough medical and nutritional assessment had been completed, Leah couldn't overload Rachel with a carbohydrate meal. Though I'd envisioned Rachel restoring three pounds a week, Leah advised two at the most. During those first three weeks of refeeding, ongoing medical assessment would be crucial. Rachel's body and mind would be treated in tandem; her body would remain at rest until some restoration occurred.

The couch-and-swing life angered Rachel. The anger of the indignant child who'd once stopped a bulldozer in a vacant field behind her house, who'd once challenged the class bully and won. Righteous anger had formerly worked but not here. Now the residential advisors or enforcers, depending on one's viewpoint, would stop Rachel from bullying herself.

"Oh, I just need a box of tissues from my room," she'd say while springing off the couch. Her jailors said no, they'd bring them to her. Or Rachel would ask to use the ladies' room. Those jailors smiled. "No, I'm sorry. You were there fifteen minutes ago."

"I can't live like this," she'd yell out. She called me at work on day three of her admission. "I hate this place," she cried. "The people here know nothing about exercise disorders and they won't let me work out like I need to."

As we spoke, I was surrounded in the neurology clinic by children who couldn't exercise much now or ever and this toughened me to my daughter's temporary loss.

"I'm sorry about this, I know it seems unfair," I said as my beeper went off. "But I'm incredibly busy. Can we talk tonight?"

"Go to your kids," she said. "But call me once the clinic ends."

Many residential centers limit the calls a client can make. Or limit their use of computers. The Center for Hope believed their clients could focus on treatment while remaining part of the larger world. A more restrictive policy, though right for some, would have been disastrous for Rachel. In those first days she called me several times. Her volcanic anger made me question if we'd chosen the right treatment center after all.

Within a few weeks, that anger morphed to despair. I'd receive early morning phone calls and hear Rachel weeping. No words at all. If at home,

I'd sit and listen. If at work I'd promise to call her back at five. "Can you wait that long?" I'd ask when stretched to the breaking point between patients and my daughter. She always uttered yes. Hearing her cry day after day during the emotional monsoon of a Reno spring amped up my long-distance helplessness.

"Can you and Dad write them a letter," she begged one evening, "and convince them that I'm not someone who can sit on a couch to get healthy. Please? You have to."

For many years Rachel had been that cheerful, thoughtful, and hyper-responsible person. I'd taken her sunniness for granted, like my own, but at some point she'd adopted my model of masking sadness with a smiling bravado. Now the two of us were exposed, raw and aching without as much as a scab for fragile protection. I hadn't yet learned what the parents of many of my patients knew: how to best listen and respond to a child's deepest pain. Instead, I reached for the nearest painkiller.

"I'll write to your treatment team tonight and fax it tomorrow morning," I promised. I wouldn't take the chance an email might "get lost." Now I could help her!

"Thanks," she said amidst her cries.

Enough was enough. Rachel's bleak mood worried me. I'd grown up with words: poetry, fiction, even the monthly vocabulary exercises provided by the good editors at *Reader's Digest*. Language mattered to me like possessions did to others.

"We should write a letter tonight," I told Mark at dinner.

"Well you write it," he said. "You'll make it sound better than I can."

We're both fans of Erich Fromm so I thought quoting him was a nice touch. Mark agreed, after all he had his medical students read Fromm.

"Who will tell whether one happy moment of love or the joy of walking on a bright morning and smelling the sunshine, the fresh air, is not worth all the suffering?" Fromm wrote.[6] Liking this passage, I quoted it in a missive I edited several times before faxing it to the Center for Hope. Just to confirm that the letter arrived, I faxed it twice.

In this ill-received letter, I said that my once bubbly daughter, and I actually used that awful word, had become tearful and depressed the past week. Were they aware of this? Being sedentary, I wrote, caused her to "wallow in her sadness." I couldn't get past myself and then offered advice. I suggested "one ten-minute walk per day" as well as allowing her to practice some yoga for "peace." I didn't specify who needed the peace.

I also added Mark's "medical expertise." Of course he didn't want her running or going to a gym, but he insisted that I include the American Heart Association's position that all adults should exercise an hour daily. He saw no reason that Rachel couldn't be out walking, like he saw no reason he couldn't complete a marathon on a stress fracture.

I hoped that Erich Fromm would sway Rachel's treatment team and I assumed they'd respond immediately to my rational plea.

They didn't.

The letter, I later learned, acquired an oh-my-God-this-mother-is-a-real-lunatic status. Imagine taking your loved one to an alcohol treatment center and a few weeks later requesting that Pinot Grigio be served with dinner. Exercise was Rachel's addiction and dressing its need in a philosophical quote didn't change the beast any more than claiming wine merely grape juice. I cringe in retrospect.

Julie, Rachel's primary therapist, eventually called me about that note. She explained that Rachel had been diagnosed with depression at the time of her admission but so far, refused any pharmacological help. Both she and Leah said Rachel needed to sit with her sadness, to consider what anorexia had taken from her. This concept widened a new lens for me. *Sitting with sadness.* I now saw time as a gift, as the substrate for her introspection. Rachel, like Mark, Mike, and me, was a doer. We were movers. On the go, the run, the snowboard, the horse; you name it, we moved. We stopped for food and sleep, the company of each other and our friends, but for the most part, we didn't stop to view the larger picture. Now that picture hit Rachel head on. She had time to understand it. So did we.

Of course she saw it differently. Only exercise would improve her mood. Raise her endorphin levels. And I, who believed in exercise as much as I did my daily rosary, one who often multitasked while trail running through the woods, had been sucked into Rachel's version of the cure. As had Mark.

Rachel lost that round. But she rebounded a few days later with one more cause for us to jointly complain about. The poor quality of the food absolutely disgusted her. Did we understand that she was stranded in some piss-poor place that had the audacity to serve cheap and unhealthy processed foods? If her father and I could see those meals we'd transfer her to a better place.

Once again, we were duly concerned. The staff forced her to eat white bread. They served nonorganic chicken and turkey. Some food even contained high fructose corn syrup, the stuff of gas and stomach bloating. And then she spotted the ingredient that sent both her and Mark spinning. Trans fat in the cheese spread. I figured out the problem. Leah didn't understand how the meals she planned were actually prepared by the cook. Perhaps the cook didn't read labels, the way Mark did, when she shopped; perhaps she didn't really understand nutrition. Oh no. Obviously I needed to double fax another letter regarding the food.

I've always been a slow learner.

This time Leah called. You could tell by her critical tone that she considered Mark, Rachel, and me all raging head cases.

"Do you know?" she said briskly, "that your daughter is *afraid* of almost all food? My goal is to show her that food won't kill her. She's terrified of carbs, especially ones made of white flour. We allowed Rachel to write a list of six foods she couldn't possibly eat. Well, that was a problem as there are only six things she will eat." Of course, I thought. Eggs, poultry, fish, yogurt, fruits, and vegetables.

I cringed. They didn't know Rachel back in her food-loving days. They only knew this version, but with her bones poking through her skin, her hair lining the sink, the staff said in unison, *You will eat everything you're served. And you will lose your fear of food.*

If Rachel ever wanted to reclaim movement, reclaim herself, she'd restore. And with each calorie adjustment, she'd steel herself against panic and earn every privilege she could. Any backsliding would mean sitting out life on the beige corduroy couches. In those long and painful days of that first month, Rachel had yet to restore and despite a gradual intake in calories, she barely maintained her admission weight.

Leah explained why. During the refeeding stage, Rachel had become hypermetabolic, meaning her already fast metabolism was operating at an excessive rate, thus requiring more food to gain weight than a healthy person. The irony was that introducing the wrong kind of carbohydrates too quickly could induce a life-threatening refeeding syndrome.

Each day Rachel told me she'd leave at the end of the month. Each day I imagined her brain, her heart, her liver, her bones sucking up every micronutrient possible. Mark and I urged her to stay longer. So did the staff.

Toward the end of the thirty days I played the game of wicked hardball that I had in the vacant ranchland behind her Santa Rosa house.

"I'm leaving," she said for the umpteenth time.

It was late, I was tired, and my patience with anorexia had vanished. "This is your choice, honey. You're an adult. But we won't allow you to return home because you can't get the level of care you need here. And if you go somewhere else, you won't be able to get a job. You'll be broke. And I know that none of your friends will let you stay with them because they're afraid you'll die. If you leave, sooner or later you'll be living on the streets. Or in a homeless shelter."

I hated threatening her but again, I had no other choice.

"I'll stay," she said. "One more month." Her voice sounded like that of a waif trembling in the Reno twilight three time zones away.

"Rachel, you are so brave." To me she'd become a warrior. "You *will* get better."

I called the florist the next morning and sent Rachel stargazer lilies, roses, and baby's breath. For both of us, flowers were blossoms of hope.

Wrung dry from tears, Rachel entered month two of the Couch Life. Improved nutrition made its way to her brain and informed better decision-making. "I have to stay," she told us. "I'm beginning to feel better here. I think it can work." Knowing that she wouldn't bolt felt like the first tentative steps to recovery. Something else happened that month. Our phone calls now included talk of others. Ella, her roommate, had made significant progress and would be discharged in a few weeks. She'd be missed.

Only later did I know more about these two. Craving exercise, they awoke early and in between the every-fifteen-minute room checks, they'd dash into their small walk-in closet and do jumping jacks. This behavior reeks of all the secretive behaviors often attributed to those with eating disorders. However, sneaky can be viewed from their vantage. Rachel and Ella were actually hell-bent on protecting their eating disorders at all costs for they saw their eating disorders protecting them. I can only imagine these two tall women, all long arms and legs, jumping up and down together in a closet jammed with clothes and boxes. They're lucky they didn't end up with a face full of hangers.

The litmus test of their recoveries would not be what they did in public view of their therapists and residential advisors; it would occur in private. The mornings they didn't work out in the closet would be small victories.

I heard about Sonya, a young woman suffering from bulimia. "This girl is a real pain in the ass," Rachel complained. "She tells *everyone* that I dice my food into hundreds of pieces and it takes hours for me to eat. Well, what the hell does she expect? This is an eating disorders treatment center. We're all a bunch of crazies here!"

Not one to mince words, it aggravated Sonya when others poked over their plates as no one could leave the table until the last person finished. Sonya lacked patience for any "nonrecovery behavior." This included watching Rachel wrap her crushed food in a paper napkin before dumping it into the trash. Sonya reported this; Rachel had hated tattling since childhood and this rankled her as much as being escorted to the ladies' room. "Just do what you're supposed to do and I won't rat you out," Sonya said.

Sonya eventually turned head cheerleader. "You can do it, Rachel. Eat everything on your plate," she'd say time after time. Often she picked up the phone when I called. "Nancy, that daughter of yours is tough," she laughed one night, "I have to keep on her ass all the time. But I think we're making some progress."

"Thanks, honey," I answered. "And how are you doing?"

"Good. Really good this time."

The cheering she did for Rachel came harder for her.

Anita, a stunning Latina in her early forties, was also bulimic. For her, treatment meant being away from her sorely missed husband and young son. Like Sonya, Anita cared far better for others than herself. She listened endlessly to Rachel, accepted her ineffable sadness those first weeks, and then encouraged her tentative steps forward. Rachel called her Momita; she called her Rachee. A gifted artist, Anita painted boldly-colored images of goddesses, sunlight, and peace. I felt stronger by seeing them.

Rachel's new friends understood every frustration she had and like her, they'd interrupted their lives for weeks or months to find some semblance of recovery. No day came easily, but in treatment they found comfort in one another. I recalled the confrontational women in the *Thin* documentary. I heard Abigail saying how women in treatment taught each other bad habits, but at this particular moment, the Center for Hope had a fortunate mix of residents and staff. They treated one another well.

On Sundays Rachel earned the privilege of leaving the couch and attending church with a young RA. After the service ended, the real healing began. On their way home, the women stopped at Target for Diet Coke and toiletries. Diet Coke is one of the anorexic drinks of choice and is forbidden in treatment. Each Sunday, fresh from church, Rachel and Tina broke that rule. And when Rachel and I spoke on those days, I thought either spirituality or contraband had saved her. "I feel so free," she'd say. "So good." One could well argue that breaking such a rule, especially after church, was deplorable. However, Sundays lent both grace and laughter. On the other days, Rachel abided by the rules, and on all days we voiced our prayers.

At the end of Rachel's second month, I sent flowers addressed to all the women at the Center for Hope. Each one had my respect. And rather than write embarrassing letters to the staff, I wrote essays and poems for Rachel. I figured I'd lace her up with words to hold her bones together until the distant day she restored weight, the stuff of life itself.

Chapter Fifteen

Vermont, 2007

At sixty-two, my mother died far too young, but in those not-enough years together she'd aced communication. As a little girl I'd sit at the kitchen table with her. She'd sip her Maxwell House coffee, strong with a touch of milk, and I'd sip mine, diluted to caramel with a lot of milk, and we'd chat. By the time I'd become a teenager, I knew I could tell her anything. The deal, she said, was how she'd always listen as long as I spoke up. And she'd do anything "in her power" to understand me.

She valued my liberal politics for those were hers. "Liberals," she told me, "accept everyone. They're fair to everyone. They work for justice." Now in the days of Trump, her definition of liberalism remains my favorite call to decency.

Long before a national discussion of gay rights took place, we discussed homosexuality over coffee. My mother explained how some women preferred women, some men chose men, and quite frankly, it was no one's damn business what anyone did in bed if both parties were adult and consensual. To her, attraction didn't always make much sense, but love, real love, made life count, regardless of what the couple looked like.

However, such liberalism wore thin when it came to her daughter's sex life. It reassured her that I hadn't been the life-of-the-party girl like her. And for many years, she prayed that I'd enter the convent and become the grace to balance my uncle's lack thereof. But along came college. I bought contact lenses, grew my hair long, traded baggy jeans for mini-skirts, and jumped into the Age of Aquarius—and bed—with my boyfriend. In our years of conversation covering anything and everything, I wanted her to understand why I'd sidetracked my Irish-Catholic upbringing.

I thought her dentures would plop right into the Maxwell House coffee when I admitted I'd had *premarital sex*.

"Tell me once again why you're having sex with him," she cried as if I'd smashed the unwritten eleventh commandment and caused Satan to handpick his hottest coals for me. I discussed my reasons calmly even though her chain-smoking was making me cough. I reeled my story in and out, like a fisherman knowing that the big fish on the end of the line may not be that convincing once caught. Somehow we made it through my sex talk. She expressed her fear that I'd been *used*. This had not been the case at all I told her. I explained love ever so rationally because at twenty-one, I still thought love was a rational emotion.

Now, decades after my no-longer-a-virgin talk, her smoke rings still encircled me and I heard her pearly pink fingernails tapping the pine kitchen table. The conversation had changed. "I *mean*," and her ghost exaggerated that word, "I had to listen all about your damn sex life. Now it's your turn to listen to Rachel about anorexia."

Of all the conversations Rachel and I had in person, and over those distant miles, I'd never thought to ask, *Why anorexia? What does it mean to you?* I'd been blinded in the beginning, devastated later on, and didn't know these things. I could rattle off information about anxiety and obsessive-compulsive disorders, but I still hadn't heard the words that wove anorexia together, that gave them shape and context.

I needed to listen the way my mother had listened to me.

On a Sunday afternoon I went to the empty clinic to catch up on charts. The only sounds other than mine came from the kitchen ice maker as it occasionally spit out new cubes. After finishing my work, I called Rachel. Sundays were less programmed for her, a good time for real talk, and after hearing about the hot Reno weather, how she was doing, how her friends were doing, and then sharing how we were, I asked her to teach me about *her* anorexia, *her* story. "I won't be judgmental," I vowed. "Make it clear, as if you were teaching a class." I sipped my Green Mountain Coffee Roasters coffee, so much better than Maxwell House, and the few seconds that passed felt like minutes.

"You know about the running," she finally said. "It started in Australia. The beaches were so gorgeous. And each day I felt stronger and more empowered." She laughed. "Those Aussie guys were giving me lots of attention. For the first time ever I felt beautiful instead of a gawky girl taller than everyone else. It also made sense to eat a healthier diet and get rid of junk food. You and dad were so proud of me when you visited. Remember?"

Of course I did. I'm the one who said, *Keep doing whatever you are doing.*

"And Dad loved how I ran just like him. For the first time I felt like we *got* each other. I felt like he really, really respected me."

This wasn't a young woman locked in control issues with her parents. This wasn't a young woman striving to look like a model. This lifestyle screamed for acceptance, the too-tall girl as she saw herself, the failed premed student whose everyday hero happened to be her father. We thought we'd built self-esteem into Rachel's psyche, we thought she knew how much we respected her, but apparently we hadn't. Huge chunks gaped open and let anorexia slither in. I shivered.

"But when I came home, I liked my new life. I needed it. I couldn't stop running. I slowly saw myself as a better person as I lost more weight. I liked the control and the discipline. The lifestyle worked because I was finally getting the kind of grades I needed for medical school."

"Did you ever think you were getting too thin?"

"Not really. People would say things. I knew you and Dad were worried but I wasn't. I just knew I couldn't change."

"Then you lost much more weight in Santa Rosa. You became the hamster running on the wheel."

"Yeah. It's funny. Everyone thinks anorexia is about *you* having control. Or about desiring the perfect body. Maybe it's that way in the beginning but after a while *you're* the one being controlled. And you don't even see your body the way it really is. All you know is that you absolutely can't stop what you're doing; you feel like if you did, you'd have nothing. Be nothing." She paused. I heard another round of ice clink in the kitchen.

"There's something else," she said. "There's a voice that orders you around. Tells you not to eat."

"A voice?"

"Well, it's not like a schizophrenic voice if that's what you're thinking. It's not messages coming from the clouds or through walls. It's more an internal voice. A conscience. It's impossible to ignore. It's like a discipline that keeps you alive. And after a while, obeying the voice is all that matters."

"What exactly does it say to you?"

Ever so slowly she repeated the internal words chanted at our table. At her grandparents' table. ***You're as fat as a pig. You let yourself go. Look at your stomach.***

This was a sickening moment of understanding more about Rachel's illness. Why hadn't I stopped Mark and his mother years ago? I certainly didn't fear them. Oh, I'd tell Mark that his comments were rude and hurtful, but after saying that, I'd drift off to my silent place. And I'd glare at his mother but a nasty look didn't faze her. I thought I'd been maintaining peace but my peace wasn't an olive branch, it was carte blanche to what I heard as inexcusable language. Never did I see that the dust of these phrases would settle as stone in Rachel's young soul.

"Mom, do you think I'm crazy?"

It's hard when your daughter is hovering at fifty pounds below her normal healthy weight to not think that maybe she's a little crazy and you're along for the ride. But I couldn't succumb to that. "Of course not. How often do you hear this voice?"

"All the time," she said. "Sharon and Leah say my eating disorder voice is constantly fighting my normal voice. Like all day long."

"Does it feel that way to you?"

"Yes."

I asked if her psychiatrist had suggested meds because her voice seemed obsessive. Rachel admitted that Dr. Wendell had urged her to start Prozac, but she hated drugs and said she'd get rid of the obsessiveness of the eating disorder voice on her own. "You probably don't like this answer," she said.

Correct. Rachel had majored in psychology and she knew medications. She also knew that if she started Prozac the eating disorder voice would diminish. She couldn't part with that voice or with illness because they'd grafted onto her identity.

On that quiet Sunday afternoon a window opened to the dark recesses of her thoughts and those thoughts shook me. As I listened, I thought about my own eating voice, one which called me to eat every three or four hours while awake and that voice yelled loud and clear. Nothing and no one could quell it. Rachel had the same voice until an opposing drive replaced it. I could almost visualize Rachel's brain as I saw her beautiful neurons, the spaces between them filled with the neurotransmitters to communicate one to another. Due to semi-starvation, her serotonin, a potent neurotransmitter, had plummeted. The unfilled serotonin receptors were linked to behavioral changes that drove her compulsivity, and the raging compulsive voice of the eating disorder to its full velocity.

"I get it," I said slowly. "I get that damn voice and what it tells you. Write every word it says."

The Center for Hope believed that the written narrative gave insight. I agreed. Writing allows us to become cartographers, to map those immutable roads of the past, but even more importantly, to spot better roads ahead. I wanted Rachel to meet her eating disordered voice head-on and somehow, bypass it forever.

"I do write every day," she said. "It helps. But are you *sure* I'm not crazy? I meet all the DSM qualifications for anxiety. Depression. Anorexia nervosa. Even post-traumatic stress disorder. I'm not that well right now."

"Sweetie, it's a shame you majored in psych. You know too much about diagnostic criteria. Your issues are being treated; someday this will be far behind you. But you aren't crazy."

"And you aren't angry with me?"

"Hell no, and neither is Dad." Instead, my anger lashed at me.

I heard her sigh. "I'm so glad you're coming out next week. Weird as it sounds with me in treatment, we'll still have fun."

"That we will."

After we hung up, I chatted with my mother. When no one is nearby you can talk to the dead and not get the fisheye you'd otherwise receive. "I'll tell you something," I told her. "You may have thought premarital sex was tough to handle but it's nothing compared to anorexia."

A few days later Rachel called and we talked about my upcoming trip to Reno. She'd been given her first pass to leave the residence without a staff member present. We'd be allowed a few hours together. I could meet her friends, she could pee without the police listening in, and we'd go out for dinner. I could even meet Orson, an old pig who'd been grandfathered into the deal when the Center for Hope had purchased the property. She assured me that I'd love him like she did.

"We used to take turns feeding Orson but everyone else hated the job," she said.

"Why?" I asked.

"It's hard getting him to eat. Sometimes he won't leave his doghouse and if people try to pull him out he squeals like hell. But he comes out just fine for me. So I have a privilege. I can leave the friggin couch twice a day to feed and water Orson. He's really a sweetheart."

Warmth had returned to Rachel's voice. I didn't know this Orson, but already I liked him. He gave Rachel a reason to get up each morning. Yes, she still needed to be cared for, but taking care of others was a requisite for her own self-worth.

Being summer, the trip West was easy. I settled into the Peppermill Casino and Hotel, had an early dinner because I was on East Coast time, and then met Rachel at the Center for Hope. Before doing anything else, she had to attend to Orson. Not a problem, I told her, even though I'd been cooked through and through by the sun.

After feeding Orson, whom I did indeed bond with, Rachel and I drove off in her CRV. She needed a few things at Walmart but this time, she didn't race through the store like she had in Santa Rosa. Shopping a mere fifteen minutes exhausted her. Wan and shaky, she needed a nap. A year ago she'd run a 5K race and barely needed to catch her breath as she crossed the finish line. That day we'd told her that she looked just like her father. Of course she was fine. Just a year ago we said that.

I took Rachel back to the Center for Hope and returned to my room at the Peppermill. I exchanged my flip-flops for sneakers and took off. Walking through cities I'm unfamiliar with gives me a sense of that place, and with time to spend before picking Rachel up for the evening, I explored the area. A few miles brought me into a neighborhood with vacant boarded-up houses, scruffy lawns, and run-down cars parked on the street and in the yards.

In the midst of this stood a small quilting shop with a tidy storefront. I walked in and saw two women standing behind the counter. The rather quaint store had been stocked with bolts of floral cotton, skeins of soft yarns, and racks of how-to-do-it magazines. Had it been there for years, perhaps opened back in better times? Could it be a front for drugs, or simply, a desert flower poking through rough urban decay? I bought a few swatches of blue calico for a quilt I'd most likely not finish. One of the women eyed my credit card that I pulled out of my jeans pocket.

"Do you have an ID?" she asked warily.

I handed her my driver's license and she looked up. "Vermont? You live in Vermont?" The woman made Vermont sound exotic and distant. "Lady," she said, "do you know what kind of neighborhood you're in? This isn't the safest place in town. You shouldn't be here."

I shoved my credit card and license into my pocket and told the woman that I didn't carry a purse or wear much jewelry. Not much to rip off. Then I said that the street reminded me of my first home.

As a four-year-old, I pedaled my red tricycle back and forth along Franklin Street in a neighborhood fallen on its own bad times. Our crowded house held my parents, my grandparents, a foster child my grandparents were caring for, and me. My cousin and her parents visited frequently. We had laughter, abundant food, a victory garden, and safety. I didn't know the street came with a reputation; I only knew it as home. A good place. Now, with my family's existence thrown across a giant baccarat table, something that harkened back to childhood blossomed like yucca after desert rain.

Reality soon replaced nostalgia. On my way back to the Peppermill, at the edge of the downtown business district, a swarm of uniformed police officers staked out a yard with yellow crime tape. Someone had recently been shot and killed. Welcome to Reno, I thought. And wake the hell up, Nancy, and watch where you are walking. This isn't Memory Lane. Mildly lost, I soon found my hotel.

After a steaming shower, a nap, and a call home, I met Rachel at the Center for Hope. She felt more rested and looked forward to an evening at the Clay Studio, one of those paint-your-own-project places. Several of her housemates planned to join us. Generally family members weren't on this weekly outing but the director made an exception as I'd traveled so far.

The young owners of the Clay Studio greeted us at the door. Apparently they reserved every Saturday evening for the Center for Hope women and they seemed to know each one personally. Six of us sat around a large round table and discussed what to make. One woman would design and paint another plate; she'd been making place settings so that by her discharge, she'd have a new set of dishes. A few others opted to make bowls for gifts. I chose an oblong serving platter and selected a fuchsia paint, the color of the roses bordering Orson's pen. Stymied about what to paint, crafts never being a skill, I stared at the white platter. "Paint it first," Rachel said.

"After it has dried in the oven, you can add a symbol or design," Sonya suggested. "It's easy." Maybe easy for her.

As we painted our pieces we chatted like old friends. Kelly, the psychiatrist, sat to my right and mentioned how much she enjoyed my poetry.

"Oh?" I said, looking at Rachel.

Rachel grinned. "Everyone does, I've posted them all around the dining room."

I considered those pedestrian verses I'd scribbled down and emailed to her. Not the stuff of literature.

"I love them," Kelly said. Then she asked who my favorite poet was. I said Elizabeth Bishop and she said Bishop was one of hers as well. I imagined Kelly fully recovered, back in practice, and inspired by an extraordinary poet, one of the best of her times, who'd turned her alcoholic demons into lasting art.

After my platter had been fired in the kiln I gave it another look. The color came out well but I still lacked an idea for completing it. Words like love, hope, and believe abounded on the other pieces. Finally I decided on a wavy Zen-like symbol, or so I'd envisioned, but it came out more like a snake than anything else.

"Oh, Mom," Rachel lied. "That's so pretty." She sounded like me when I'd long ago complimented her fifth-grade pottery attempts.

As I sat with these women, I thought about how they were in giving professions. Anita was an art therapist, Sonya worked with troubled teenagers, Kelly had just finished her psych residency, and Rachel had taught in AmeriCorps. These women were articulate, social, impeccably groomed, and kind to a fault. On a Saturday night they should have been out with friends for dinners, movies, or parties. Instead they were recovering in Reno and painting inspirational words that they may, or may not, have believed on alabaster pottery.

At the end of the evening, I stood at the counter, paying for my snake platter. The owners of the Clay Studio, like the lady in the quilt shop, commented on my Vermont ID. "You're so far from home," the wife said. "But your daughter is in a good place. The Center for Hope is amazing. We love all their residents."

The husband looked at me, his pale blue eyes ancient in his still boyish face. "We see your daughter every Saturday night. Such a good girl. You need to believe this. The Center for Hope performs miracles."

I stood speechless. On this surreal day that included a pig struggling to eat, a walk ending at a murder scene, a snake on a plate, and now this message, I felt overwhelmed.

"She *will* have a miracle." The man spoke with such authority that I wondered who he really was. Shaman? Pastor? Seer? A chill traveled my spine. My hands trembled as I took my credit card and license from his. I squeezed tears away. My faith in miracles, small or large, had dwindled, but he had sustained me.

"Thank you," I tried saying but words clogged my throat.

Chapter Sixteen

Vermont, 2007

Staying alive can exact a harsh toll. Mark's dad, Joe, urged Fran, Mark's mom, to start treatment, but Fran had said no, but maybe later. Pancreatic cancer, often so quickly fatal, just poked away at her. Eighteen months into her diagnosis, Fran finally consented to surgery. In the month following my Reno trip, Mark and I visited New Jersey twice. As a doctor's son, Mark knew no limits. He'd contacted one of the top pancreatic cancer surgeons in the country and scheduled appointments with him. Joe relaxed; we had positive motion, a real plan, and an October surgical date at the University of Pennsylvania.

We often asked Fran how she felt about this. She'd lift her eyebrows and say *who needs it* and each and every time, *That darling Rachel should get better fast.* Fran spoke readily about a new movie or play she'd seen or a new restaurant she'd been to. I knew every detail of the relatives' colonoscopies or dental implants. And she regaled in bar and bat mitzvahs and what dresses she'd wear. But when it came to her own health she shut down. No, not many people knew she had cancer; she'd told a few she had some ongoing stomach problems. I winced, knowing I'd be acting the same.

Now August, time of swampy New Jersey weather, we switched gears and focused more on Rachel. Rachel's team suggested an entire family visit and therapy session. We liked this idea, though sitting with a therapist, our problems exposed like nerves with their myelin protective sheaths stripped away, seemed daunting. In preparation for this visit, Rachel implored us to please, please act normal in Reno. I asked her how much normal she meant; a full one hundred eighty degrees from normal with plenty of leeway, or something smaller, say, thirty degrees of normal.

The teacher's voice came out. "All of you need to act really normal. No leeway whatsoever."

Albert Camus, one of my heroes, put it another way: "Nobody realizes that some people expend tremendous energy merely to be normal." I had a significant worry. Perhaps one or two of us might not expend any energy at all in that normal direction.

Besides, with Fran and Rachel so ill, closer to normal happened in the past. Not now. Rachel had been at the Center for Hope for three months. Some weeks she restored a pound; other weeks she lost one. Her hypermetabolic syndrome burned on. Each week Leah increased Rachel's daily calories, but that weight gain I imagined at admission never occurred. Rachel admitted serious ongoing conversations with her eating disorder voice. Depression wore her down; anxiety cranked her up. Every Thursday morning Rachel's team held a conference regarding her care. Afterwards Leah updated me. Her honesty generally disheartened me and I needed snacks both sweet and salty to make it through the day.

"Your daughter is so frustrating!" she said on one of those Thursdays. We'd just finished the morning clinic. I stood in the employee lunchroom with potato chips in hand as staff wandered in and out. Sun lit the room, the Green Mountains a dense, summer backdrop twenty miles away. "She's just about the sickest of the sick I've treated in twenty years! Do you have any idea how stubborn that girl is?"

Like I hadn't seen Rachel stop bulldozers, avenge school bullies, question school administrators? Though stubborn, Leah said she still finished her portions each day. But it took a huge effort.

"When do you think she'll finally start restoring?" I asked. "Maybe in a few weeks?"

"Perhaps months."

I tried absorbing that fact. "So I guess, I guess we should prepare ourselves financially for this," I said, wondering where the money would come from. Rachel torched calories; we'd emptied our savings account for her costly treatment.

"Prepare yourself for the long haul."

My beeper went off. The text flashed the patient's name and message regarding a three- minute grand mal seizure. I thanked Leah and said I had to run, but we'd prepare. I returned to my desk, flipped the computer chart on, and called the patient's mother. I'd left my own situation for that of another and for the next fifteen minutes worked on that problem instead of mine.

Flying from Burlington to Reno is a series of puddle jumps, and four flights later you're just happy to be on the ground for a few days. After we landed we rented a car, and picked Rachel up as she had a two-hour pass to help us get settled at the Peppermill. As we walked through the casino on the way to the registration desk, I knew I'd be playing later. Like my mother often said, life is a crapshoot. I imagined a windfall, a tidy sum to pay Rachel's bill.

The hotel registration lines were packed eight people deep. After four flights, standing in line didn't appeal to me, especially since my legs ached from being folded into short people's seats. I asked Mark to please get us a room, any room would be fine, and I'd just wait with Rachel. Looking at her weakened me. I'd fervently hoped for even a small weight gain since I'd seen her the month before. No. She remained just as gaunt as on the day she'd been admitted. I felt limp, not as in fainting but as I must park myself immediately. There were no available chairs so I flopped right onto my suitcase. This might have succeeded if I had a full-size suitcase rather than a twenty-one-inch carry-on, but physics didn't come naturally to me. Of course the little suitcase collapsed and sent me sprawling. All my bleary eyes could see were hundreds of chandelier lights glaring down at me. In downtown Reno, only the bright, the garish will do.

Being on the floor might have appalled some, but I laughed. Rachel did too. No one else shared our inappropriate laughter but we weren't dissuaded. Mark heard us and turned around.

"Can't you act like a normal woman?" he whispered severely. "Do you see anyone else falling off their suitcases?"

Rachel's laughter sounded like hitting the jackpot so Mark's understandable disdain didn't bother me. Rachel scanned the reception area with one hand arched above her eyes. "No," she deadpanned. "I don't see anyone falling off their suitcases except Mom."

I hauled my weary self up and joined the line with everyone else. It took us another fifteen minutes to get to our room. And what a room.

We opened the door and were welcomed by that unmistakable odor of old smoke unsuccessfully masked by air freshener. Tinted glass mirrors hung on deep purple walls and a super-sized California king bed dominated the room. I pushed a button and a flat screen TV rose from the credenza at the base of our bed like a sea monster emerging from the deep. The bathroom, and here we certainly got our money's worth, outsized our dining room at home and contained a massive hot tub bedazzled with gold-trimmed mirrors. And for the lady, a lovely bidet and a white telephone awaited her.

I explained bidet protocol to Mark and Rachel. "It's important to keep your knees together," I said knowingly, "because in the last casino I stayed in, I neglected to read the instructions. I got a face wash rather than a bottom one." Rachel laughed and asked if her dad knew that story. I said yes and it didn't surprise him.

As I looked around the suite I doubted how we'd sleep in the stale smoky room but why worry? Mark and I didn't sleep well anywhere. Rachel didn't know we'd become raging insomniacs and we weren't telling her. Already she felt guilty about the cost of her treatment. Knowing that we whispered *will she live through this* at three in the morning would be far too much weight for her broken self to carry. So rather than discuss these matters with her, I played the giggling clown about my fancy bidet facial. Rachel's laugh, those sibilant notes from her better days, had definitely returned. Maybe she'd follow it.

We relaxed in the suite for another twenty minutes before driving Rachel back to the Center for Hope. Late that night we headed into the casino. I appreciate casinos because they are usually accessible for those with disabilities. As a neurology nurse I admire the accessibility of a building like others admire architecture. It saddens me that our public libraries, churches, temples, and restaurants often lack decent ramps, wide hallways, and adapted bathrooms. The casinos run on the premise that the dollar is the common denominator and at the casino, money crosses gender, age, race, and disability lines. However, despite accessibility, the casino is the real home of the Heartbreak Hotel. You can read desperation on the faces of those hungry to win, and no doubt we looked desperate too as we sat at the poker table. As we'd soon remortgage our home and take out a large personal loan, we needed God to deal our poker hands.

We got stuck with the regular dealer. By midnight I'd won only twenty dollars. Down forty, Mark said it was time to leave but I wanted an early morning breakfast on my winnings. He reminded me that I shouldn't sleep on a full stomach and I reminded him that I couldn't sleep on an empty one. It never fails to amaze me how long-term partners can keep on suggesting the same things. After his initial grumble, Mark scarfed down oatmeal and blueberries and I enjoyed the comfort of eggs Benedict, a half plate of home fries, and a side of fruit.

We slept five hours in the smoky suite, a long night for us. In the morning we stood in line for the breakfast buffet. "Nancy," Mark warned, "don't stuff yourself. We're taking Rachel out for muffins in a few hours and then we'll have a big lunch at noon."

"Don't worry," I said, my eyes darting along the buffet counters. Though winning comes hard at a casino, there's always a payback with food. I filled my first plate with fruit and yogurt, my second with plump sausage links, crisp bacon, and Belgian waffles, and my third with scrambled eggs, buttered toast, and a few more of those tasty sausage links. How my father would have liked this breakfast with us, how I'd grin and say, *I sure inherited your appetite*.

My first coffee hadn't worked but the second delivered quite the jolt. I felt like Super Woman after so much food and caffeine. I could take on any day.

After breakfast we circled back to the airport and picked up Mike. Now in a graduate environmental marine biology program at Western Washington University in Bellingham, Washington, Mike hadn't seen his sister since Christmas. Though slender then, she didn't look unhealthy. Now she did. We'd noticed how people stared. No, gawked. Some no doubt made fun of her. Or us. We'd warned Mike about her appearance but his face registered shock and devastation when he got out of the car and saw her in the Center for Hope parking lot. Rachel ran to him, wrapped her decimated arms around him, and wept against his chest. An old image came to mind. Rachel following Mike up the apple tree in our Pennsylvania backyard and getting stuck fifteen feet above ground, him backing down to her branch and leading her foothold by foothold to safety. Now, when she needed him the most, the footholds were distant and their navigation almost impossible. Still clinging to Mike as they got in the car, Rachel wiped her eyes. "I have a five-hour pass," she said. "I've never been away that long. Let's get the hell out of here."

Leah mandated our first stop would be the coffee shop. She'd warned Mark over the phone that we'd eat just as normally as Rachel needed to. There'd be no chatter about cholesterol, calories, no judgment about the sizes of the other customers. For thirty minutes Mark would forget his Doctor Heart Healthy persona. She didn't remind me of anything; I'm a muffin lover, the bigger, the better. Same for Mike.

As part of the Center for Hope's philosophy, clients frequently enter the real world of eating out as opposed to being cloistered in the treatment center. Rachel and her housemates went out for coffee and muffins twice weekly. Once a week they went out for lunch and dinner.

"Unfortunately, we drive the waitresses crazy," Rachel explained as we waited to place our orders in the coffee shop she frequented. We faced the glass display of rich pastries and thick sandwiches, and I hoped these would trigger her hunger. "It's not a pretty sight watching women cry in public because they have to eat," she said. "After all my catering work, you know how I feel about treating waitresses. So I just swallow my food even though it gags me."

Mark stared down those muffins like they were assassins. Jumbo sized, puffed out beneath a dome of crystallized sugar, some bursting with blueberries, others oozing chocolate, those goodies hit Mark hard. I took his hand. "Don't you dare order the fat-free one," I said.

"We can't act like we're afraid of food," Rachel growled.

Then it was time to order.

"Be brave," Mike said to his dad. "It won't kill you."

Against what I knew to be his better judgment, Mark ordered the regular chocolate chip muffin. I sighed in relief and the rest of us ordered the same way. My casino coffee had fizzled out so I drank another to jettison me through the day.

We found a table and I tried ignoring the onlookers Rachel seemed oblivious to. My hurt from those stares never abated. Sure I sat straight in my chair, pretended all was well, but sadness suffused each breath. I wanted to hit everyone looking our way.

Rachel ate mechanically but at least she didn't push the muffin around her plate or pulverize it with her fork. I called that improvement. This ranked up there with the day she toddled forth on wobbly steps. How we'd clapped for her back then and how she'd smiled back.

"I like how you ate that muffin," I said. "It's a good start for our day."

I didn't say, *Thank God Mark ate the muffin that would potentially plug his coronary arteries or bloat his stomach.* Nor did I mention that he'd scooped up each morsel as if manna from heaven after trudging on foot across the Continental Divide.

After this snack we drove to Walmart, a mecca for Rachel. Here she could buy moisturizers, hair products, and perfume. Here she could see women's magazines, their glossy covers signaling success and how to attain it. *Be your best this summer. Lose ten pounds in two weeks. Find new confidence in your toned body. Ten exercises that will change your life.* Those glossies suggested that abs of steel and a sculpted butt would ensure happiness and a better life. Look at the airbrushed models on these magazine covers. Look at their smiles as they radiate self-esteem in their size two bikinis; surely, they found the right path. *You can be your best self yet,* one cover promised.

Most women bypass these magazines; some linger, purchase, read, and actually benefit from the articles. Some find the prescriptive diets and exercises unrealistic, and forget them. And then there is the subset of women like Rachel for whom those magazines rouse their eating disorder voices, call out for an inhuman perfection, and they answer. They diet more compulsively, or eat and purge; they run more miles, pump more weight in the chase to perfection.

Rachel would have been only too happy to buy a magazine or two, but at the Center for Hope, as well as at most treatment centers, these magazines are equated with illegal drugs, laxatives, and cutting instruments.

"Contraband," Rachel said longingly as I directed her to the safer shampoo aisle. Four weeks earlier Rachel had been dizzy and fatigued on our Walmart trip. Not now. Despite no discernible weight gain, she'd become stronger. A good sign for our day and now I fully expected that lunch would be a success. I knew Rachel wouldn't disappoint Leah or trouble a waitress. Perhaps she'd even enjoy her meal rather than robotically swallowing it down.

Leah had stipulated that lunch be close to noon. We'd be eating at the Stone House Café and Rachel had agreed to eat a turkey sandwich on whole wheat and eat every french fry accompanying it. By noon, none of us were hungry due to those five-inch-wide muffins. However, we'd agreed to an on-time lunch so we went to the restaurant.

The Stone House Café had a relaxed summertime feeling and as the coffee shop had gone well, I thought we'd also feel relaxed and summery here. Rachel, lacking body fat and always chilled, chose a patio table in full sun. I prefer shade, especially when jet-lagged, so I pointed to a round table beneath a wide umbrella. Rachel graciously acquiesced to my preference.

During college I worked as a barmaid. While taking orders I could spot the fussy, the indecisive, the impatient, the big drinkers, the fast talkers, and the entitled. Worst of all, I could guess who the miserable tippers might be. How people ordered food and drinks, used or abused them, and how they interacted with those at the table, and with those waiting on them, opened a wide lens into their lives.

Our waitress at the Stone House Café had a real education coming her way thanks to the Levine family. Rachel, as prompted by Leah, placed her order for the turkey sandwich with fries. Calorie-laden carbs were as crucial for her as the protein-rich turkey. This had sounded good to us until we'd had our muffins but now, not so much. The waitress, assuming we were all there to eat, asked what we'd like. Mike, with his aw-shucks smile, decided he wasn't that hungry yet so he'd have a chicken Caesar salad. Mark agreed that this sounded great and he'd have his with vinaigrette, please, on the side. Like a kid, I always want what the other person orders and so I abandoned my turkey sandwich and fries for my own chicken Caesar. The waitress smiled as we were an easy table. So far three salads, one tray, and a 20 percent tip from the smiley family. No doubt she assumed the ultrathin girl wouldn't order much.

Rachel's face crumbled. "I can't do this," she cried, "I have to get out of here." And she took off.

"Hold our orders," I told the surprised waitress. I chased Rachel across the crowded patio and caught up with her as she sobbed against the low stone wall bordering the dining area. If we were providing drama for the relaxed summer crowd I didn't give a rat's ass.

"What is it that you people don't get?" she asked. "You aren't supposed to come here like you have eating disorders too. We're all supposed to have something with carbs. Not just me!"

I hugged Rachel and told her how sorry I was that we blew it. The apology fell short. She pulled away and sprinted toward our rental car, the running addict sentenced to a couch, her white skirt billowing around her stork legs. Even out of shape, she beat me across the long parking lot.

"We have to go back," I said as we leaned against the hot car. "We'll just order right this time."

"I don't care that you and Mike asked for salads. And I heard how well you ate at the buffet this morning. It's Dad! He's afraid of the fries. He's as rigid about food as I am."

"I promise you Dad will order the right way."

We made our way back to the table amid the usual glances or frank stares and I politely coached Mark how to reorder.

"Rachel is the one with the eating disorder," he said with the conviction of an innocent man being wrongly accused. "There's no reason to raise my cholesterol so I can have fries along with her."

"Just do it," I hissed as the waitress approached the no-longer smiley family.

This time around we all requested the turkey with the fries and Rachel asked for mustard instead of mayo on hers. The waitress smiled and said of course, no problem.

Our food arrived in record time but once again, Rachel's voice broke as her shoulders slumped inward. A goopy layer of mayo coated her turkey. Not good. Rachel cried again; we signaled the waitress and explained the issue. The waitress remained upbeat and helpful. She'd return immediately with another sandwich. Rachel thanked her through her tears.

Five minutes later the sandwich arrived but Rachel could only eat a few bites. Like the other women in treatment, she too had wept in a restaurant and how she hated this. The waitress asked if there was anything she could do or get but we said no. Those of us eating finished our meals and we tipped the waitress 50 percent. She'd earned it.

Leah suggested that after lunch we take a short walk at a nearby park. The temperature, according to our car radio, had risen to ninety-five degrees. The cloudless sky, a blinding blue ceiling straight to Sacramento and beyond, beat down in a way Vermonters find lethal. The sun, the fiery heat, and my own bloated stomach didn't mix so I found a rustic bench under one of the park's few trees. "I can't move," I said.

I'm not a whiner. I pride myself on not whining, not whining even in childbirth, but at that moment, I'd damn well earned whining rights. My once healthy daughter had lost one-third of herself. Her life, like ours, had been suspended. I despised anorexia, but I also hated the burning sun, the insufferable heat, and the way I'd gorged with midnight breakfast, the morning buffet, an enormous muffin, and of course, the turkey special.

In twelve hours I'd consumed so much food that I saw myself as one of those tasty sausage links ready to burst through the skin. After all my coffee, I wasn't just jolted, I was fried. I hadn't slept through the night in months, my ankles were still water balloons after four flights, it had risen to ninety-five-hundred degrees, and my people, the Irish, perished in this weather.

"Listen up," I whined and whined well. "I feel absolutely gross from all I've eaten. I'm too sick, too stuffed to move. And I'm about to fart my brains out so you had better back away."

Rachel's eyes were tracers on mine. "I know," she said. "I feel gross every time I eat. I'm forced to eat so much now that my stomach aches constantly. I feel horrible almost every minute of the day. I feel like a bloated pig. Welcome to my world."

Perhaps one of the strongest connections a parent can make with a child is that sustained look into each other's eyes at a moment of total understanding. Language, at least in words, isn't necessary. I now felt as Rachel did and she knew it. Our smiles met in air so hot that they shimmered on the dizzying waves of August.

"Don't worry, Mom," Rachel said. "You rest here and Dad, Mike, and I will keep going."

"Good idea," I panted.

I watched the three of them walk shoulder to shoulder across the scorched lawn. We'd failed the normal test yet again, but regardless, after ten minutes of shade and several good belches, we'd be on our way together.

Chapter Seventeen

Nevada, 2007

After our colossal failure at the Stone House Cafe I had every reason to think our first family therapy session the following day would be like group root canals done without pain meds or dental insurance. My hands shook as we drove to our appointment and my antiperspirant had already failed on another blistering hot day. We passed a hillside charred from a recent wildfire. An ugly sight, though at ground level pale green shoots vied for light and moisture. Seeing those scarred areas made me long for Vermont, and made me wish yet again that none of this had ever happened. As if a mere wish could retroactively change history.

We were scheduled to meet Sharon, the family therapist, and Rachel at 11 a.m. "Please don't be late," Rachel pleaded over the phone. "We acted like idiots yesterday. Today needs to be better." Well, I thought, no matter how bad this gets we'll at least be in an air-conditioned room.

Mike and I exchanged awkward looks for we, the private ones, felt squeamish and weren't saying much on the drive there. Mark filled in our gaps with his talk. He looked forward to this session. It would be a great time for us to better understand Rachel. As a doctor, he'd recommended family therapy many times and he'd always seen good results. He clearly lacked the stomach-clenching worry Mike and I shared. On the ride to the Center for Hope, Mike and I were sweating but Mark, the cool and far-from-private one, said he had nothing to worry about.

Five minutes before eleven, and uncharacteristically on time, Mark, Mike, and I entered the all-purpose room on the second floor of the Center for Hope. Rolled yoga mats lined the beige walls and yet more plush beige corduroy couches and overstuffed chairs faced one another.

Early as we were, Sharon and Rachel awaited; Sharon with a warm handshake, Rachel with hugs. Sharon emanated a gracious and caring professionalism. She too signaled confidence.

Sharon invited us to sit down. Rachel took the chair closest to hers, Mark and I sat side by side on one of those oh-so-comfortable couches, and Mike took a nearby chair. Sharon thanked us for coming and supporting Rachel. She also thanked Rachel for the privilege of working with her and getting to know her better. Then she looked intently at each of us.

"Today is all about Rachel," she said. "Rachel has many things she needs to say to you and this is her opportunity to do so."

Rachel sat close enough to Sharon that if need be, Sharon could lean over and touch her shoulder. Rachel also thanked us for coming. Her quivering voice became a plangent cry that filled the room. Hearing her made me gasp. Sharon gave Rachel time to compose herself. She looked at Rachel and then again, at the three of us.

"We are not here to talk about the past," Sharon said in a nonjudgmental tone. "Instead we are here to start over. We have a new beginning with one another this morning, and to do this, there are several things Rachel must say."

I liked this approach and sensed that it was well rehearsed.

"Mark," Sharon said kindly, "Rachel wishes to speak with you first. There are issues with you that she feels impacted her eating disorder. When she finishes speaking, we invite you to respond. And then, a little later, we'll talk more with Nancy and Mike."

Rachel separated her tears from her voice and began. Pain tightened those words into little fists. "You need to know how much I love you, Dad," she said. "How much I admire you. And there's no one in the world I respect more."

Mark nodded.

"But I felt like I never measured up. Didn't work hard enough, didn't want medical school enough. I felt like I'd let myself go. Like I'd disappointed you when all I ever wanted was to be like you."

Mark tried to interrupt, to refute her words, but Sharon asked Rachel to continue on. Rachel spoke for several more minutes. She then left the past behind in Vermont and spoke only of the present and what she needed from him now. She needed her dad to act like a normal person, one without his own eating issues. She needed him to enjoy running but not be a running freak. She needed him to refrain from talking about people's weight. Or their work ethic. They had much to work through, she said in her shaky voice. The plan was that the two of them would do family therapy every week, via phone, with Sharon. "Can you do this?" Rachel asked. "I can't change if you can't."

Mark likes quoting the American Heart Association's guidelines recommending that adults exercise a full hour daily and eat a heart-healthy diet. I assumed that he'd politely and rather professionally remind Sharon that he was only following these guidelines. The problem rested with Rachel who'd pushed her lifestyle out of bounds, to a dangerous and obsessive place that had nothing to do with him. He'd suggest that perhaps starting Rachel on Prozac would be far more effective than putting him in family therapy.

I called it wrong. Mark is an articulate speaker in either a small room, a large auditorium, or even on TV. He's never without words or with big hand swoops accenting those words. Until that day I'd never seen him mute; I'd never seen his hands still.

"Dad," Rachel asked. "Can you do this?"

Mark nodded as his skeletal daughter requested that he make a profound change in his attitude and in his life. Okay, he sounded demented in the supermarket as he criticized the various would-be killers on the labels of food products. Sure he'd been the masochistic runner who completed a marathon on a stress fracture. And let's not forget his responses at the Stone House Café. But years back this man had been so worried that his baby daughter might not wake in the morning that he'd slept for months with his hand on her tiny chest to monitor her breathing.

"Rachee-poo," he said as if incanting her childhood nickname to cast a wellness spell, "I'll do whatever it takes to get you better again."

I saw Mark catch his ragged breath the way Rachel caught hers. I'd never witnessed greater humility or grace in him as he leaned forward to his daughter, his face grave, his Adam's apple rising and falling, his fingers clenched.

I knew Mark would carry out that promise for he's a man who honors his word. However, I'd predicted a different response. I'd expected him to say yes, he had high standards, but only to instill a work ethic in his children. And granted, he'd say, he might have discussed food and exercise too often, but he maintained a high bar regarding a healthy lifestyle. Instead, he stunned me by agreeing without question or comment to Rachel's wishes for their future. For her he'd change. For her, whatever it took, he'd do it. If I'd been a bride carrying a crystal ball instead of white roses, I'd have seen this moment. No way would I have walked down a candlelit chapel aisle to him on our wedding night. I'd have run lickety-split into his waiting arms.

Sharon knew where to break the tension. She thanked Mark and turned to me. She'd heard that I was Rachel's role model for eating and also heard that I'd knock down old ladies if one stood in my way at a lunch line. I laughed and said I did like to eat on time. Kind of like my horses wanted their grain delivered at the expected hour.

Sharon then explained that the focus of family therapy would be centered on Mark and Rachel. Would this work for me? Did I need professional support?

I only needed Rachel to be well again. I confided in Mark, my close friends, my coworkers, my father, my cousin, Bentley the dog, and even in my horse.

"I'm well supported," I said.

Sharon smiled again and said that she had some good news for me. Rachel had shared that I'd always been the family negotiator. The mediator. Now that she was the family therapist, I could resign this role.

We all assume a specific role in the families we come from and in the ones we make. Somewhere back in my own childhood I'd found a certain success as a peacemaker. I'm not sure when or why this happened. Perhaps it had something to do with my slow fuse and the fact that I read constantly. In the midst of an argument I could sound level-headed, rational, and with luck, halfway intelligent. Gradually this peacemaking mission imbued my personality.

I remained a negotiator and peacemaker in college, later in my work, and finally in my own family. Around the house I was Little Miss Fix-it. I'd explain how the thirteen-year-old Rachel had annoyed her brother by screeching Hanson songs. I'd explain how the twenty-one-year-old Mike wished to be with his friends and not have his younger sister tagging along. I'd make nice when Mark came home tired and grouchy from a long hospital day; and I'd apologize when I turned up late for another school concert or game. It seemed that in the midst of all my explaining and pacifying, I couldn't even tell time. Fatigued from years of making the peace, I knew I hadn't done a fabulous job because here we sat with our hearts in our throats in a Reno treatment center.

"I'd be happy just being a mother and a wife," I told our group. "I'm tired." A fifty-pound weight dropped from my broken chest.

I'm sure Mike felt the same weight slip off him when Sharon said that she understood him to be a very good brother, and that nothing he'd ever said or done had impacted Rachel's eating disorder. She added that from time to time, she'd include him on a family phone call but at this point, she hadn't scheduled anything; however, he could call her if need be. Sharon also asked that he remain in close contact with Rachel. Mike thanked her. I didn't think he'd call Sharon but I knew he would call and email Rachel often.

At the end of our session, Sharon once again shook our hands. Rachel hugged each of us, a hug that to me felt like sadness and joy, despair and hope, anger and forgiveness. Her heart pounded within the frail cage of her ribs and I prayed that it would carry her through.

This meeting is grafted into my memory. Never did anyone blame or judge Rachel for her illness. Never did anyone blame her family. Instead, Rachel asked her father to make certain changes along with her. Mark's utmost commitment to doing so made for one of the most endearing and respected moments of our marriage.

How fortunate we were to be in 2008, in a time when parents were no longer being blamed for their children's anorexia. Research yielded new answers to causes. An increasing number of family, twin, and adoption studies had provided data that genetic factors contribute to a predisposition for developing anorexia. In addition, neurobiology and neurochemistry research has indicated that those with anorexia have differences in brain structure, dopamine and serotonin regulation and their effects on mood, and ghrelin and leptin production, the hormones controlling appetite. The question is what came first, the horse or the cart. Did the anorexia cause these changes or did they preexist the illness? Follow-up studies of those recovered from anorexia will provide future answers as well as target the most optimal treatments.

Families don't cause anorexia but we are in a prime position to alter its devastating effects. We could work alongside Rachel and improve our own attitudes about exercise and food. We could alter the passed-down language of *fat as a pig* or *letting herself go*. As a family, I knew we'd be respected and supported at the Center for Hope.

I can't imagine the pain families endure when they are ascribed blame by the medical community, or from other family members or friends, who have outdated views on this illness and its causes. Sometimes I'd laugh when I heard these viewpoints. I'd think to myself that if families caused anorexia we'd be a country of pencil-thin citizens.

Parents who now hear such blame or condescension should politely hand that person current research papers for his or her immediate edification. Or, as we say at work, stick it where the sun won't shine.

Chapter Eighteen

Philadelphia, 2007

One month later Mark, his father, and I sat in the surgical waiting room of the Hospital of the University of Pennsylvania. Fran, now eighty-five, had agreed to the Whipple procedure, an extensive surgery targeting pancreatic cancer. Every hour a nurse came to update us. Each time we received the same good news: the surgery remained uneventful and Fran had stable vital signs.

Early that evening we visited Fran in the surgical intensive care unit. We assumed she'd look ashen and be groggy, the things expected of a patient her age, especially one who'd been harboring cancer for eighteen months. No. Fran had good color and was alert. She didn't even complain of pain, just mentioned that her midsection felt stretched. "I'm tired," she conceded. "Why don't you kids and Joe go out for a nice dinner?"

We settled for the hospital cafeteria so we could be nearby in case she needed us. Joe and I ordered burgers but Mark, not finding anything heart healthy, had wilted greens topped with what looked like canned fruit.

Fran's rapid recovery from a complicated procedure stunned us. She had no immediate post-operative issues and two days later, sat ramrod straight in a bed on the surgical unit. The Whipple procedure can down a fifty-year-old but not my mother-in-law. We should have videoed her first time up for hospital public relations. Fran slid to the side of the bed, leaned slightly on her nurse, and then transferred easily to a chair. She wanted water. Her teeth. Her wig. We smiled in awe.

Fran sat comfortably for a half hour before Mark's younger brother, Steve, arrived from Queens. Such a thoughtful gesture, I thought, to wear the T-shirt he'd bought at the Catskills resort where we'd celebrated Fran and Joe's fortieth anniversary. He no doubt assumed this seventeen-year-old shirt was a reminder of good times. Unfortunately the T-shirt had shrunk since then and he had expanded. Steve said a quick hi to us and went straight to his mother. Bending over, he kissed her cheek. Fran appraised him with one of her piercing looks. I feared the worst.

"You shouldn't wear that old shirt," she said. "It's a rag. And you should do something about your stomach. It's gotten really big."

My voice escaped like a starved tiger springing from a cage. "You will not," I yelled, "ever talk to anyone about his or her stomach again! Or their size. Or weight. Do you, do you understand what I'm saying?"

Fran looked at me and cocked her eyebrows. "Of course, darling," she said mildly.

Softening my tone, I turned to Steve. "You're fine just the way you are. And thanks for coming. I know it's a long trip in beastly traffic."

Fran's nickname had long been the "Queen" and I, one of her royal subjects, had waited over twenty-five years to defy the crown. Like I couldn't have found a more appropriate time? Did I need to loudly criticize a frail older woman so soon after surgery? My parents would have been appalled by my lack of respect.

As we ate in the hospital cafeteria that night, Mark congratulated me and said I should have done this long ago. Steve mumbled something about his mom "always saying things like that." Joe said he hadn't turned up the sound on his hearing aids so he'd never even heard me. Regardless, I wouldn't have changed a word. At the same time, I now understood how the importance of weight and appearance had been drummed into Fran, how her thoughts about them were as pathologic as Rachel's. I couldn't fault her any more than I did Rachel. Nor could I any longer blame Mark for parroting back every comment he'd grown up hearing.

This I knew to be true: for better or worse, we often sound exactly like our parents. Being angry with any of us, myself included, would have been useless. As Sharon so wisely said, *We are moving forward; we are dealing with today and the future.* Moving forward meant *all* of us using the right words. As for Fran, she never spoke about weight or appearances around me again.

I imagined Mark's grandparents, young immigrants at Ellis Island, marrying, starting families, and dollar by precious dollar, moving from poverty to the middle class where discrimination against Jews would last for another generation. No wonder *appearances* mattered, no wonder anxiety flourished, no wonder Fran's own mother inculcated her with the importance of *looks*. I knew that we were the next chapters of a generational story but the time for serious revisions had arrived.

These came about at what felt like the speed of a glacier. Rachel continued her intensive therapy and gradually absorbed the truth about anorexia. Rather than protecting her, it had robbed her body and mind. Yet as hard as she fought to get rid of anorexia, the voice of her eating disorder grew louder. As the weeks wore on, her calories were increasingly bumped upward, yet still, no weight gain. Between the demands of her eating disorder voice and her hypermetabolic syndrome, nothing she did felt enough.

"So how much are you hearing that voice now? I asked one evening. I'd assumed that she had *some* kind of life away from its obsessive call.

"Like all the time. Every day. Every night. It's pretty much all I think about."

"I had no idea. This is horrible."

"Yep."

"I know you hate meds but if you don't start Prozac you will grow old at the Center for Hope."

For weeks, Leah, and Sharon had pushed her to begin medication. Rachel's response had been that she didn't like chemicals in her body. True. She didn't even wear makeup because she liked being natural.

But I knew a few discrepancies. If allowed, she'd sprinkle Splenda in her coffee and chug Diet Coke. *Some* chemicals she approved of. Her voiced reasoning about Prozac was partially true. The real reason went deeper; Prozac would diminish the obsessive control of the eating disorder voice.

"You really think I should start meds?" she asked. "I know you hate that stuff as much as I do."

"Yes. Your brain needs a rest. It's exhausted."

The next morning Rachel agreed to start medication and she laughed, saying that Dr. Wendell had cheered for her. So did Mark and I. Now Rachel had fit the last piece of a complicated puzzle together and could move on to the next one thousand pieces of her life.

On Friday afternoons, Sharon, Rachel, and Mark had their one-hour therapy sessions via phone. Rachel and Mark shared their challenges, and how many there were, about broader diets and less exercise. Rachel had signed a contract about this upon admission.

Mark had signed his own while visiting the Center for Hope. He'd limit running to three days per week. He'd add certain foods back into his diet. Endorphin starvation was one thing, but the concept of eating butter and dessert threw him into a heart attack panic. Rachel feared calories, Mark feared sudden death, but their conversations weren't angst filled. Handling their demons together brought levity. And for me, pride; pride in the work they were doing, and how they were doing it together.

"We're both crazy," Rachel told me one night. I heard a modicum of pride. "I feel less guilty now. I don't feel like I screwed up so much."

"There's nothing to feel guilty about at all," I told her. "You never screwed up. And it's amazing how much you and Dad get each other. You two are impressing the hell out of me."

"I guess I was kind of a sitting duck for becoming anorexic."

"I think so. But you're getting better."

We knew our family genetics; the anxiety and OCD, traits on Mark's side demanding perfection in academics, in work, or in appearances, the same ones on my side often leading sooner or later to a bottle of something, anything. But we recognized a truth more powerful than all our negatives. We came from people who had had survived potato famines, pogroms, two world wars, plus a Depression, and we were raised with the belief that family had each other's backs. We were in it together, maybe patched with Gorilla Glue, but together. Imperfect yet perfect.

Each week thousands of words substituting for an embrace, words offering understanding, hope, and the promise of a better tomorrow flooded our phone lines and kept us within reach. Weeks ran into months and we alternated focus from Rachel to Fran, then back to Rachel; this set the rhythm for a dance we barely knew the steps to. Yet we learned them.

I'd too often noticed how neurological and psychiatric issues unraveled many of the families I'd known through work. Close to unraveling ourselves, the time had come to emulate the successful families I'd known, to practice the lessons they'd been quietly teaching me over the years. Love the child you have, not the vision of who you thought your child would be. Get all the help you can drum up, for grit alone won't carry you through the day. Find time for your partner or spouse, for the lack of time together will erode a relationship. Make the medical system work for you and push harder if it pushes back. Sleep when you can. Eat well. Be with those who support you and steer far from those who are negative or toxic. Make time for your own needs. Communicate with yourself, your partner, your medical support staff, and most importantly, your child. Or young adult. Keep moving forward; pray hard and then twice as hard. And practice the helpful modality of crying in the shower.

Those Friday afternoon calls with Mark, Rachel, and a gifted family therapist did move us forward. Kept us together like our families before us. Sharon capitalized on every strength Rachel and Mark had. Never did she point the misshapen finger of guilt or failure. As a result, father and daughter worked on what was authentically healthy for both of them. Sometimes I'd sit in Mark's office during a session and I'd hear laughter. Those two could crack each other up and they did the same for me.

Rachel and I talked most days. No longer sentenced to a couch, she practiced yoga. Took evening walks. Hung out with her new, and what would become lifelong friends. Twice daily she fed and watered Orson. Caring for him filled her need to be productive. Even on the tougher days, and they remained numerous, she had someone besides herself to think about and do for. Pigs, even the fussy Orson, got hungry.

And one day, she did too. Her long-deadened appetite, though far from normal, reappeared. A gift, this call to life.

Slowly she learned the art of being gentle with oneself. Rachel had goodness and kindness for all, but during her illness, a punishing discipline took over. In its wake was left a woman threadbare of pleasure. Rachel needed to relearn that a full stomach felt good, not gross, that a massage felt comforting, not merely indulgent. Most importantly she learned that she deserved a good life. A mindful life.

Like all illnesses, the course of anorexia remained uncharted and unpredictable. Leah continued to call every Thursday morning regarding Rachel's weekly team meeting. Some weeks Rachel had restored a modest few pounds so she'd earn a privilege. Maybe a short hike in the foothills. Or trail riding on a slow and bombproof horse. Other weeks didn't go so well and Rachel chafed at losing a privilege.

"Will she ever gain weight consistently?" I asked during one of those calls. Again I stood in the not-so-private employee kitchen. By now, the whole staff knew Rachel's story and rooted for her.

Leah didn't sugarcoat one word. "I have no idea," she said. "She's still suffering from hypermetabolic syndrome. And her eating disorder voice is powerful. Rachel's actually one of the toughest patients I've ever dealt with."

Yes, weeks before, she'd called Rachel the *sickest of the sick*. That girl of ours had never done anything half-assed.

Each week Rachel's calories increased. She surpassed three thousand calories per day. Then four thousand. Finally five thousand. Rachel resented so much food. She complained of severe stomach pain, bloating, and constipation. I remembered feeling that same way in the broiling hot Reno park. Yes, eating can hurt. We cheered her on. We cheered us on.

In mid-October, the Vermont mountains burned orange, scarlet, gold, and tourists drove through them at turtle speed. I stared at those mountains, my pastime during the Thursday updates, and wondered when we'd ever get a positive call. One that would send me hopping up and down with joy the way Rachel did when she'd been accepted into AmeriCorps. I ticked off the five months of inpatient treatment and knew she'd need more. Somehow, we'd provide. We'd blown through our savings, remortgaged our house, and needed a large credit union loan to cover the remainder.

Every Thursday during lunchtime, our credit union rep, a slender dark-haired woman, set up shop outside the hospital cafeteria, that being the best time and place for staff on a short lunch break to meet. After that disquieting call with Leah, I stopped at her table even before checking out the daily special. I requested a large loan and explained all the reasons why. So much for privacy as people passed by.

The rep smiled up at me. "You borrow as much as you need to get your daughter well."

I thanked her and said that she had no idea how much this meant to us. We'd be good for the loan. We'd work years and years to repay it. We weren't leaving town.

"Get her well," the rep said and handed me the loan application. The credit union processed it immediately; we'd have all the money required for Rachel to finish her treatment. As we signed the promissory notes, I knew our good fortune to have stable professions. I considered those parents who couldn't pay the steep bills of residential treatment once insurance ran out. How cruel to have an illness not well reimbursed, how unfair for parents to sink into behemoth debt if outpatient or home-based programs don't succeed. No wonder anorexia carries a greater than one-in-ten mortality rate.

Leaves bury most of our yard in late October. Raking them takes days of drudgery, but not so that year. Each leaf I raked felt like yet another calorie for Rachel. Now at five thousand calories daily, she ate three enormous meals plus three large snacks. To Bentley and me, this task spelled paradise, but for Rachel, purgatory. Her stomach pains and misgivings never waned.

I raked on. Hours of physical work relaxed me. Beneath the slate autumn skies, the scent of wood smoke and wet leaves permeated the crisp air. I could have hired myself out to the neighbors.

Rachel's eating disorder voice: *You pig! They're making you fat and lazy here. How can you sit at the table and eat two plates of food every meal? All you do is eat. You're gaining weight nearly every week. Look at your stomach. It's no longer hollow. You're disgusting. And when they hand you a six-hundred-calorie milkshake for an evening snack, take it out to the swing. When no one is looking, water the flowers with it. Stay smart here; don't listen to these people, don't give in.*

Chapter Nineteen

Vermont, 2007

The epic battle of Rachel vs. her eating disorder voice continued and I'd grown so used to Leah's frustrated updates that my platitudes eased them. Of course it could be worse. *What if Rachel stopped eating? What if she signed herself out of treatment?* The week before Thanksgiving I stood in the employee kitchen and looked at the bare trees as I dialed the Center for Hope.

"You'll be very excited when you see Rachel at Christmas," Leah told me that day. "She's restoring nicely. Finally."

I wanted to break out in my happy dance. We'd spent almost six months waiting to hear those magic words and after the call, I immediately called Mark.

"You won't believe this," I sang. "Leah is actually positive today. Downright cheerful, and she even used the words, *restoring nicely*."

"Thank God," Mark said slowly, savoring Leah's words. "It's about time. All those calories had to catch up with her at some point. Hard to believe it's taken so long. I can't wait until we see her at Christmas."

Sharon had coached us about the upcoming trip. In her supportive but certain voice she reiterated Mark's exercise and eating contract. If he couldn't honor it, there would be no blame placed on him. However, Rachel couldn't come home until he followed every rule.

"It's like I'm evil," Mark said. "Like I'm the one who could ruin Rachel's recovery. All eyes are on me. I'm the bad guy."

"You've never been the bad guy," I told him. "No one at the Center for Hope has ever said that. And neither have I. But they've talked about some habits they asked you to change. The fact that you're dealing with them is incredibly brave. And besides, we both blew it in some ways."

I didn't hide from my culpability. Neither did he.

"But the good news," I told him, "is that we never meant to screw up. But we did. So we changed things for the better."

"I feel like we'll be under a microscope when Rachel is home. Like Sharon and Leah will be checking in every day to hear how we're doing."

"They'll call. You can count on that."

Mark threw his hands in the air. "God, I hate Christmas. All those goy things. And now the food police are calling. And by the way, if I hear one more Christmas carol I'll vomit. It's only November and that's all you hear in the stores."

"Settle down, Baby Cakes. This Christmas will be special. Rachel is finally restoring some weight. Mike will be home. And Jimmo and Phyllis are coming."

I knew my dad and stepmother would be easy company.

In the past year I'd racked up too many brittle moments in airports and on planes. So many arrivals and departures wrought with fear after seeing Rachel. As I waited for her plane to land on a late December night, I paced the airport shops. Bought magazines. Water. Decaf. Made phone calls. *No, she isn't here yet. Any minute though.* Finally I stared out a broad window in the observation area as her plane touched down: perfect landing, plane skimming across the tarmac, braking, and stopping. The jetway connected to the plane's exit like an umbilical cord. I held my breath as I left the observation area and approached the gate. All those hard months of not knowing how any of this would end. *She's restoring nicely*, Leah had said. Those words became my favorite Christmas lyrics and I'd never tire of hearing them.

Rachel finally emerged from the throng of holiday travelers passing through the gate. Never shy of the public spectacle, we galloped toward each other. *Don't you dare cry*, I lectured myself. *You might not stop. Just take a deep breath and remember this moment forever.*

There she stood. So present. So healthy. Yes, slender. But nothing about her appearance belied the past year. She looked younger than twenty-three, fresh-faced, almost carefree as if life had been one long holiday. We hugged. Enveloped in a midst of woodsy Burberry perfume, I felt real flesh. *Do not cry*, I ordered. *Not here. Not now.* My arms held that one-time bruised newborn who'd lost her heart rate prior to delivery. *You look so beautiful*, I'd said that day.

"You look so beautiful," I said in the airport. "I can't believe how healthy you look!"

We spent the afternoon decorating the tree, making gingerbread cookies, playing Christmas carols, and talking. We didn't run out of words to describe how pleased we were, how healthy Rachel was. She'd been in treatment for seven long months and the enormous space and privacy of a real home seemed a luxury. She felt entitled just walking into an unlocked bathroom.

One could argue that Rachel had restored enough weight to be discharged. However, Rachel's team had warned us that her eating disorder voice would quickly convince her that she could have it both ways; eat just enough to look healthier but remain subservient to the demand of exercise and food restrictions. They predicted relapse with an early discharge.

I'd told Rachel, and anyone who cared to listen, that I positively, absolutely, unquestionably could not handle a relapse. Not to make her feel pressured, but I said, a relapse would kill me. Simple as that. Not an option.

"I'd like to stay home," Rachel wished aloud while we were making dinner. "But I know it's too soon. I'm not ready."

Restoring more weight would improve Rachel's brain function, aiding and abetting the long-term recovery I needed as much as she did. As the Center for Hope had gotten us this far, we all agreed to extend Rachel's time there. I called the Center for Hope the best graduate school she'd ever attend.

How not ready for discharge she was became apparent in the dining room. Rachel ate well. Nothing remained on her plate and her portions equaled mine. However, I ate with the abandon of a hungry golden retriever; she ate dutifully, as if doing algebra problems. The Chunky Monkey ice cream, her all-time favorite dessert before anorexia took her away, went down like rat poison. But she finished it.

We'd neglected to ask Leah or Sharon if we should comment on how well she ate. Would this call more attention and undermine her effort? I voted on how Rachel made me feel.

"Seeing you finish your dinner makes me happy," I said. "I know it's still not easy for you."

Rachel nodded.

Mark smiled at her, one of his big congenial smiles, the kind Mike had inherited. "I'm proud of you," he said.

I was proud of him for not droning on and on about the heart-healthy diet. I didn't say a word, though I longed to say several, when he ate dessert just like a normal person. I wanted Rachel to think it wasn't an act at all, just our ordinary family dinner in our candlelit dining room on any old Vermont winter night.

After dinner Rachel called Janna, a housemate at the Center for Hope and her designated support person during this week at home. Getting through dinner hadn't been easy for Rachel. Janna understood every nuance of this experience. She urged Rachel on just as Sonya had done months earlier. I'd met Janna once at the Center for Hope. We'd sat together on the kitchen bar stools, eating freshly baked cookies, and she wore killer high heels, the kind I'd break a leg in. One of her parents had been invited to join family therapy, just as Mark had. The parent declined. Janna called Mark a hero and I'd agreed.

Jimmo and Phyllis arrived on December twenty-third and later that day, Mike did too. Good conversation with plenty of noshing prevailed. If we skipped the part about Rachel's anorexia we were quite the celebratory group.

Though Christmas remained Mark's least favorite holiday, he reserved all comments about the saccharine monotony of Christmas carols and the expense of gifts. He approved of our tree; a straggly thing bought half-price earlier in the day. The kids decorated it with their longtime ornaments: thumb-printed miniature trees etched on construction paper, gold star-shaped cookies that held up through the years, little bears wielding hockey sticks, angels galore, tiny silver bells, blown glass orbs, and white crocheted stars. Though hardly a designer tree, once we flicked on the white lights, the leftover tree shone.

I'd made spaghetti and turkey meatballs for Christmas Eve dinner. We gathered at the dining room table, said a tepid grace because we weren't the praying out loud kind of family, and ate heartily. I wanted to shriek, *Rachel's eating pasta, Rachel's eating pasta!* But I deferred. She knew when I smiled her way that eating a bowl of pasta, an anorexic toxic carb, made my evening. And she smiled right back.

After dinner we did a group clean up. Several obsessive compulsives made for a tidy kitchen. My father kept an eye on the clock so we'd be early for Mass. He hated arriving later to find the back pews, his favorite place, already filled. We stomped into church in heavy boots. What an eclectic group we were: my devout Catholic father; my Methodist stepmom, one who didn't brag about good Christian acts but did them daily; the hybrid Cashews, what Mike called the Catholic-Jewish kids like Rachel and him; the reformed Jew and my lapsed Catholic self. I elbowed Mark hard so he'd listen to the carols with his best manners. Filled with gratitude, I appreciated every part of the Mass and, deep within that lapsed Catholic, remained the choir girl who still believed in the church and the sacraments.

Just like life on a Hallmark card, snow fell lightly upon us as we drove home. As a special treat for my father I made oyster stew, a long-time Christmas Eve tradition that my mother had honored. She'd always insisted on using cream and butter, no heart-healthy substitutions for her. My oyster stew tasted as good as hers, so good that my father and I each had two bowls. And we chased this down with eggnog, bread, cookies, and potato chips.

"Now Jimmo," Phyllis reminded him. "You know how you get with oysters. Perhaps you should slow down."

"I'm fine. And I'd like a little more stew before going to bed." And there went his third bowl.

We heard Jimmo vomiting in the guest bathroom that night. "This always happens after my dad's annual reunion at the power company," I told Mark who wondered if we should check on him. "He eats too many oysters, gets sick, but is better the next day."

In the morning my dad vomited blood so we set off to the emergency room. After a panel of thankfully normal lab work and six hours of intravenous fluids, Jimmo looked quite well. He promised he'd never eat oysters again but I knew, come summer and reunion time, those succulent oysters would have their way with him, and once again, he'd be sorry.

Later that afternoon we opened our Christmas presents. Every year Rachel insisted we do this *exactly* the same way. First we built a fire. Next we pulled the green leather couch and the pine rocker close to the tree. Finally Mike, the official handler of gifts, passed out presents one at a time. Instead of big gifts, we gave each other Darn Tough socks, books, CDs, and Lake Champlain chocolate bars. We wrapped these presents in gleaming holiday foil with personal notes taped to each package. Again, gratitude filled me, my thanks spiraling inward, a quiet benediction following desperate times.

Our best gift sat by the tree. Rachel shimmered like the white lights, the silver and gold wrapping foils. Such incandescence I could only dream of during the past months. My father, chagrined by the oyster episode, sipped herbal tea and ate saltines as we finished opening our presents.

Rachel reveled in her freedom, especially using the unlocked bathroom without someone listening in. The ultimate freedom came a few nights after Christmas as she and Mike left for a party. The rush of a night out, just an ordinary night with friends, turned her cheeks pink. She'd missed these times.

The Center for Hope ran like a convent. Women lived communally, followed strict schedules, and devoted themselves to a cause but rather than religion, recovery, an altogether kind of soul searching, prevailed. Men lived outside the house; they figured in the past, perhaps the future, but certainly not in daily life. Rachel had once told me that the only man she'd seen inside those white walls was the carpet cleaner guy, though she'd been there so long she'd seen him several times. Seeing men again would be even more liberating than peeing in private. Part of me wanted to shout warnings. Don't drink too much. Be sure to eat. Don't smoke a joint. I wanted to tell Mike to protect her but I knew he would.

"You guys have fun," I offered ever so casually as they put their boots on in the mudroom. "See you in the morning." I guessed they'd be out late. I wouldn't wait up for them per se, maybe just read in bed until I heard their car pull into the driveway.

Like her grandfather, Rachel overdid a good thing while celebrating. Well before dawn I heard someone enter the guest bathroom and start vomiting. I knew it to be Rachel; just by their footsteps I can identify my kids. Most parents have this inborn skill.

"Well," I mumbled to Mark. "This should complicate her flight today."

"You better check on her," he said while transitioning from night to day in a blink. "Find out if she got drunk. See who she was with."

"No. I'm going back to sleep for a few more hours. You should too. And if Rachel drank too much this is a lesson learned." I shut my eyes. So many lessons my family kept learning.

Pale and tired, Rachel ate eggs, toast, and turkey bacon two hours later. "I can't miss any meals," she said with a lame smile. "I mean I had two margaritas last night. My liver sure isn't what it used to be."

As we packed for her trip back to Reno, Rachel talked more about her good time. She'd seen Sam, a sometimes love interest over the years. "We made out," she giggled like a giddy teen.

"And?"

"Just to kiss a guy again felt incredible. I forgot how good it was."

I thought, *Shut the hell up, you eating disorder voice, and let a twenty-three-year-old woman enjoy this pleasure. Let her enjoy a kiss. Or more.*

"But next time I go out I guess I'll have only one drink," she said.

"Definitely."

My father shared his concern. "Not a good sign," he told me while Rachel went upstairs for her suitcase. "She couldn't control herself at a party. Someone on pass from treatment shouldn't be drinking. How can she be trusted?"

I knew my father's fears. I'd had decades of hearing about my uncle and his weakness, my uncle serving time in Attica. Hopeless my uncle, and of course the slur, *The Irish are no good.* Even worse, I recalled the times he'd criticized my mother for her drug dependency, how he worried that I'd become like my uncle or her, and now he worried that Rachel would.

"You better watch her," he warned. His tense expression and hand tremor interpreted his version of the ongoing family story.

I unplugged the Christmas tree lights before leaving for the airport and the holiday ended.

Rachel's eating disorder voice: *See what happened to your grandfather? Ate too many oysters and wound up in the ER. Gluttony all right. And look at you. Eating all the time. You're out of control again. If you were smart, you'd get discharged now, before it's too late. Before you gain any more weight and look just like Orson.*

Chapter Twenty

Vermont, 2008

Winter bore on and Rachel gradually restored more weight. In addition, she gleaned how her very temperament had set her up for an eating disorder. She knew she couldn't alter that but she could develop coping mechanisms to deal with anxiety and obsessiveness.

I had my own coping mechanism. Nearly every morning Bentley insisted upon a three-mile lap around Shelburne Bay. We navigated the icy trails but sometimes I slipped, landing face first on frozen tree roots. I'd lie on the ground, push back up, and think, yes, this is what we do. Keep going. Crash a few times. Snowflakes chilled my tears. On the winding, heavily wooded trails, I'd say a rosary. In return for my imperfect prayers, the silvered trees bent their bare limbs around me.

In Reno, Rachel learned mindfulness. In the woods, I did. Together, we bided our time.

During these months of Rachel's improvement, Fran's illness followed a different trajectory. Chemotherapy and radiation exhausted her so she spent her days sitting in a comfy chair by her bed. Joe maintained a drill sergeant mentality of keep marching and never give in. Therefore, every few hours he'd haul Fran out of her chair and walk her around the house. He swore that eight trips through the rooms plus her physical therapy exercises would make her strong again. During a late winter visit, we heard them arguing.

"I'm not moving," she shrieked while we pretended to read the paper in the family room.

"Oh yes, you are," he yelled back.

Without his hearing aids tuned up, or even on, Joe didn't hear himself the way we did. I'd study their wedding pictures hanging on the bedroom wall, the ever-so-chic couple in their fitted 1950s suits, and measure how love had morphed.

"Why are you doing this to Fran?" I asked.

"You guys don't get it," Joe explained. "I have to keep her moving to keep her alive." His energy and passion for keeping her paralleled our own with Rachel. Still, Mark and I questioned Fran's quality of life.

One afternoon while Fran napped we sat in the living room, the room only used for company. We felt like trespassers. Sitting in one of the gold velvet chairs, I asked Joe if he thought more chemo was in Fran's best interest.

"Don't tell me the alternative!" he barked back. "A woman from a nursing agency came to do a home health evaluation. She gave me some crap about end-of-life care and I told her to get the hell out of this house and never return."

So we asked Fran if she wished to continue treatment. She swept her hand outwards and said what we knew she'd say. "Who needs it? But Joe says I should do it."

Mark and I finally understood the dynamics of their fifty-seven-year marriage. Fran chose the restaurants, the vacations, the movies, the gifts, and there wasn't much give and take on her part. Joe made the financial decisions and the health directives. Likewise, not much room for disagreement. He said keep fighting and she did.

The Fran I'd known precancer complained bitterly about a broken fingernail, the wind tousling her teased hair, a waitress forgetting the lemon for her water. But give Fran major surgery, six months of chemo and radiation, and she didn't flinch. She didn't vomit. She didn't complain of pain. Each month more weight slipped away, but she kept going. Her white blood cell counts stayed relatively stable and she never caught a virus, let alone develop sepsis as many cancer patients do. It seemed that the DNA dance down the double helix had lent Rachel some of her grandmother's survivor genes. Both kept going in the muck of life and how I admired them.

By early March, nine full months after first driving to the Center for Hope, Rachel had fully restored her weight. She'd earned every possible privilege she could. Daily therapy continued and each day she wrote journal entries, some brief, others longer and given to serious introspection. Twice daily she cared for Orson, a chore she never tired of. Still hypermetabolic, she continued to need fifty-five hundred calories daily and Leah had no idea when this might normalize. Oh, how I wished I needed that many calories. Due to such good nutrition, and to Prozac, Rachel's serotonin levels normalized; thus, her obsessive thinking declined. She couldn't fully escape the muffled hiss of her eating disorder voice but now she could stamp it down. We dared to envision a realistic recovery.

Rachel had qualified to live in the Center for Hope's transitional living program and she'd moved to an apartment a few miles away. She returned each day for therapy but she shopped for all her groceries, prepared her meals, was on the honor system regarding exercise, and to her delight, could use the bathroom without a guard. Such transitional programs give one a better chance at a sustained recovery and after her rugged course, we all voted for this.

During these weeks, we discussed discharge planning. What kind of aftercare would be available? Where would she live? Who would she be living with? When would she resume working? The first step would be homecoming; Rachel yearned for Vermont and we said yes, yes, come home. She couldn't wait to hike up Mt. Philo, to feel the rush of the breeze through her hair at the summit, to look across the lake to the jagged Adirondack peaks. She longed for coffee on our back deck, for watching the warblers darting between the tall hemlocks enclosing our yard. As for work, she thought she'd work with kids, her passion, and though she loved Orson, she missed real children. After a year of lost wages, she also wanted to earn money. Regaining independence meant everything to her.

After those first few months with us, Rachel thought she'd move to Denver and share an apartment with Emma, her close friend from fourth grade sleepovers, class trips to DC, and high school classes and sports. They called each other sisters and long ago had vowed that someday they'd live in a big city together. Emma had spent a weekend at the Center for Hope to learn how to be the best possible roommate for someone recovering from an eating disorder. Emma, like Joy in Santa Rosa, had a big heart and eagle eyes. If Rachel's recovery wavered, even though we said it wouldn't, Emma would call us immediately.

As for work, Rachel had a nebulous idea that she'd find a teaching job within a few days of landing in Denver. If this didn't pan out, she'd nanny or do respite care. We knew she'd be safe with Emma, and we knew she'd find work, but the prospect of her moving far from home again unsettled us. What if her recovery wasn't quite as assured as we hoped? However, discouraging her independence troubled us too. So we honored friendships with women like Emma and took a scary leap across our chasm of fear.

Sharon and Leah thought these discharge plans reasonable. Phew. Sharon suggested that Rachel see an eating disorders therapist three times per week and she'd initiate a plan to ensure continuity of care. This made sense from my nursing point of view and I saw no barriers to setting this up. Amid doing barn chores late one afternoon, I took a break and called a highly recommended therapist in Vermont.

"Yes," she told me. "I treat women with eating disorders but I can't possibly see a client that frequently. Someone needing such intense support needs a different structure than I can provide."

"Do you know someone who can?" I asked, leaning against a stall door and getting my hair gently mussed by a horse demanding attention.

She recommended a therapist almost an hour away. We'd been hoping for someone closer so I called another one. "Oh," this nearby one said. "Ten months in treatment? My goodness. I don't treat women who have been that ill. Best of luck to both of you." Three more therapists turned me down and then I remembered why I love horses. They rarely disappoint me.

The following day I drove to an office and did what I often tell the parents of my patients to do: If you aren't getting the answers you need, show up at the doctor's front desk. Refuse to leave until someone either pays you the right attention or security hauls you away.

Ever so politely I told my plight to the receptionist, one who actually made eye contact and smiled. "We'd love to have your daughter as a patient," she said warmly. "But we don't have room in our schedule to see a client three times a week. That's a bit unusual."

I retold my story in a louder voice. I'd noticed a blond woman sitting in a back office and guessed she might be the therapist. I wanted her to hear my desperation. To my relief, the therapist, Sarah, invited me into her comfortable office. She offered me tea or coffee. Her dog, an immaculate white puff of friendly bichon, sniffed me over before vaulting onto my lap. Obviously, the dog did her own therapy as she cuddled against my chest. Our family story splashed out fast and dramatic with me saying that Rachel must have three sessions per week for her first month out of treatment. Someone had to accommodate her. Sarah and the dog had the situation under control.

"Not a problem," she said. "Of course I can see Rachel that often. I'll call the Center for Hope and begin her transition plan immediately."

I could have hugged Sarah but petted her fluffy dog instead. I knew they'd be the right team.

At the end of March I visited Rachel. No longer did her hair resemble Orson's. The dead ends had been trimmed and the new growth came in soft and shiny. The Nevada sun had tinted her pale cheeks and nothing about her conveyed a recent catastrophic illness. Best yet, according to Leah, she'd reached her goal weight though neither Rachel nor I knew the exact number.

Rachel's nemesis and then cheerleader, Sonya, shared their transitional living apartment. Sonya had been home for several months but relapsed. This time, she thought, recovery would last. On my second night there the three of us went to the movies. As the girls stood in line for buttered popcorn, I hung behind and admired them. They'd weathered ordeals but their resiliency matched their difficulties.

Never has popcorn tasted so good, the sweet warm butter coating the hot salty kernels, the large-sized bag enough for all of us. Watching them eat equaled my own pleasure in eating. Most likely I was the only person in the theater thrilled by watching her companions eat popcorn.

"Do you believe this girl is going home?" Sonya asked as we watched the coming attractions. "Her recovery better stick. I think it will though."

"I hope so. I'm not sure I have it in me for a relapse," I said.

In private later that night, I told Rachel we had no more money for a relapse either. We hated pressuring her, but she must understand that going backwards wouldn't work. Besides, I had extraordinary belief in Rachel, just as I did when her heart rate had plummeted for those long eight minutes prior to delivery. That day I thought, *I couldn't go home without a baby.* Twenty-four years later I thought, *Rachel is better. She can't relapse.*

You'd think the memory of all those anorexic months and the severity of Rachel's illness might have left me shaky. Instead, feeling both relaxed and jubilant, I rode a good wave. I met with Sharon, Leah, and Dr. Wendell for one final time. Sharon remained ever professional: warm, communicative, and positive about Rachel's move home. She thanked Mark for all the work he'd done; I thanked her for rebuilding our family. We were lucky to have her guidance through a year of Nevada wildfire.

Leah's crisp military bearing skidded right into warm and fuzzy. You'd have thought she birthed Rachel herself. And then led Mark to the straight and narrow path away from orthorexia. "You know what this is?" she asked me. "It's a miracle. Look at her."

I nodded, too overcome to say those words myself. I couldn't imagine Rachel dropping contact with Leah and neither could Leah. We decided that for a while, she'd remain Rachel's nutritionist via weekly phone calls. Maybe, we thought, for at least a year. Or forever, if need be.

Then came time to say goodbye to Dr. Wendell, to thank her for her extraordinary program that saved our daughter. I recalled the day a distraught Rachel couldn't make her therapy session. Dr. Wendell went to Rachel's room and held her as she wept because anorexia had become her profound grief.

But before I could thank Dr. Wendell, she thanked Mark and me for trusting her, for handing Rachel over for ten months, and for making the changes at home that would ensure her recovery.

Finally, I went to the kitchen and thanked Ayisha. Like the day we arrived, the scent of freshly baked chocolate chip cookies filled the room. I sat at the counter, munched on one, and thought of all those hard days Ayisha nearly spoon-fed Rachel. And then on those better days, I saw the two of them hip-hopping across the floor, making far too much noise for those working in the nearby office. I promised to encourage Rachel to name a grandchild after her.

"It's definitely not a Jewish name," she laughed and gave me a bountiful hug.

Minutes before leaving, I sat for the last time by the stone fireplace, by those huge windows looking upon the futures of those struggling within. The women gathered there wished me luck and said how Rachel inspired them. I hugged each one and wished her the best. "All of you deserve to get well," I said. "You're amazing women." One grinned and said I should write a book about our experience.

"Maybe," I told the group.

After so many goodbyes and embraces, Rachel and I walked outside to where a cab awaited to take me to the airport. We waved to Orson who of course had no idea how monumental the day was. On a day of hugs, hugging Rachel goodbye, her body, a real body to encase her bones, felt like a multimillion-dollar jackpot.

"Can you believe I'll be home in a week?" she asked.

"No."

"Leaving here will be the best day of my life. And one of the hardest too."

We looked back toward the white house, the porch swings at rest on the wide porch, the rose bushes soon to bloom.

"I couldn't have made it without this place. And you and Dad and Mike."

"We couldn't have made it without you."

So marked my last trip flying from Reno to Phoenix, Phoenix to Philly, and Philly to Vermont. I'd crisscrossed the country for two years and in the infinite space between the heavens and earth, clung to Rachel and our family. As I flew eastward that morning, I felt as if I could touch the sunlit clouds fanning my window. I'd grown up in a faith where those needing a serious miracle or two made a pilgrimage to Fatima. Instead, we traveled to Reno, the tawdry aging sister of Las Vegas, our journey's end to a holy place named Recovery.

AFTERWORD

LOVE AFTER LOVE

The time will come
when, with elation
you will greet yourself arriving
at your own door, in your own mirror
and each will smile at the other's welcome,

and say sit here. Eat.
You will love again the stranger who was your self.
Give wine. Give bread. Give back your heart
to itself, to the stranger who has loved you

all your life, whom you ignored
for another, who knows you by heart.
Take down the love letters from the bookshelf,

the photographs, the desperate notes,
peel your own image from the mirror.
Sit. Feast on your life.
—*Derek Walcott*

It's good to know the devil you're arm wrestling with. As excited as we were about Rachel's discharge, the work of recovery would be ongoing and at first, ever so fragile. We knew her eating disorder voice could rage back and in case I needed reminders, several well-meaning folks told me the horror relapse stories of their friends or loved ones. *This will not happen*, I told myself as part of our ongoing story.

But this story of recovery is far more Rachel's than mine; it's the ongoing narrative of her trusting her own resilient voice to quell those sirens of subtraction wailing in the distance, to sit with hard-won elation and feast on her good life.

OH, THAT FIRST YEAR
by Rachel Levine-Spates

I remember hearing several people say that if you can make it in recovery for seven years, you're pretty much in the clear and that your brain will have formed enough new connections so your chances of relapse will all but diminish. The first year that I was "out"—code for no longer within the safety of the treatment center—I couldn't even imagine how I'd make it one year.

Yes, I had that joyous and hope-filled departure from treatment and I owned all the tools needed for recovery, yet I still feared the realities of living a fully recovered life. At that time full recovery meant me never thinking another eating disordered thought and being completely typical with food and exercise. I remember meeting people who were in recovery while I was in treatment and thinking, *This is so cool, they really did it*, though feeling on a deep level that there was no way I could ever get to such a place.

People define recovery differently, but my favorite definition came from Dr. Wendell. She shared with me that "recovery is not the absence of thoughts; it is the absence of behaviors." This made tremendous sense and opened my mind to the *possibility* of recovery. I believed that I could (maybe) get to a place of not engaging in behaviors—but I was never sure that I could get rid of thoughts altogether. This definition offered hope.

We had always said as a family that relapse was "not an option," something I believed and felt on a visceral level. The relapse rates for anorexia are very high and as someone who gets easily romanced by fear—I had to try not dwelling on that for it would undermine my efforts and be fodder for my eating disorder voice to again take over.

At discharge I was still hypermetabolic, and consuming at least fifty-five hundred calories daily felt daunting. Fighting the shame that the eating disorder wanted me to feel while eating large plates of food proved a real challenge. While in treatment I'd grown accustomed to eating what I needed, but the new context changed everything. Being home with so many memories of restricting and overexercising, and then doing things differently to have a fighting chance of recovery, was quite tricky. I had to form new associations with eating and ignore old behaviors with food and exercise. Despite the reality that eating and moving my body differently would save my life, my eating disorder brain felt disappointed. And the eating disorder voice was still so loud that bringing my comforts from treatment associations to home associations proved crucial.

Much of the first few months of recovery *had* to look like they did in treatment so I could have a shot at success. I met with a therapist three times a week, weighed in twice weekly, and ate the same high caloric diet I needed. Physical activity remained quite restricted except for yoga and short walks. I still needed to discuss my thoughts around food and to reconnect with those lost cues of hunger and satiety, cues very disjointed in people with anorexia. I needed to be most open about all my feelings and commit to this even when I knew how crazy I sounded to others! I especially needed to name my actual fears and anxieties so they wouldn't morph into me fearing food and what it might do to me.

Creating this treatment center-like home environment with supports in place helped my transition feel smoother. After several months I'd maintained full weight restoration and Leah gave the okay to move to Denver, as laid out with my posttreatment exit plan. I'd be moving in with one of my closest friends from way back in fourth grade and we knew Emma would be as supportive as possible. She'd keep me on track. After much planning and excitement, my dad and I left on our road trip to Colorado.

We had a contract that we'd created as a family, and I kept this in my purse to serve as a constant reminder of what I must do. In it my expectations were typed out and loosely included the following: must maintain weight, must continue weekly therapy, must care for myself appropriately and honestly, must be mindful of exercise, and must do what Leah asks. If I broke the contract, I'd leave Denver immediately and return to Vermont. I revisited that document many times that first year when my eating disorder voice grew loud. (Note: the contract stayed in my purse for years and years because it became such an important part of my life and my commitment to recovery.)

The first year was hard. I was still on a very limited movement program, still hypermetabolic, and still trying to make sense of life without an eating disorder. The work I did in treatment around the *purpose* that the eating disorder served was crucial. I needed to return to this so I could get those needs met *without* relying on eating disordered behaviors. If I was feeling fearful about the future, or out of control, or like I wasn't "enough," I could pick up the phone and talk about it or sit down with someone who understood—so that I wasn't alone with the toxic thinking that made me want to disconnect with myself and connect with the disorder. I could go for a short walk or hike or listen to music. I could journal or meet a friend for coffee, and interrupt that thought process through redirecting my energy elsewhere.

This wasn't easy to do and I couldn't have done it without several pieces in place.

First, I had to maintain complete weight restoration so that my brain could function more lucidly. Simultaneously, I needed to continue the Prozac I'd started in treatment to ensure that my brain chemistry wasn't an additional barrier. Lastly I had to do the daily work of therapy (group, individual, and family) to learn and relearn in some instances different ways of being and thinking that produced more recovery-minded results.

I remember meeting Leah a few months after arriving in Denver. She was in town visiting family and I joined them at a restaurant. That night I ordered chicken, vegetables, and rice and proceeded to pick at my food and undereat. Afterwards, Leah said that she was horrified by my poor attempt at eating. I knew I could have eaten much more as well as ordering something far more adventurous than plain old grilled chicken. I knew I'd screwed up and that this meal served as a wake-up call. Leah said that things better change immediately or my days in Denver were numbered.

That's how easy relapse can be. A few less-than-optimal meals. And then a few more after that. In the blink of an eye, it's a dozen.

Thankfully, I corrected my course, but that moment clarified my understanding of recovery. Recovery is a choice every single day, whether you are on day one or day two thousand. You must choose recovery to experience recovery. It doesn't happen by accident.

There's no magic potion that cures an eating disorder and I realize that what worked well for me might not work well for someone else. We each need and require different things at different times. Over the years it's been important for me to revisit the list of nonnegotiables that I created while in treatment. This list includes things like: under no circumstances will I weigh myself or look at my weight if I'm being weighed at a doctor's office; I will always eat those three appropriate meals each day as well as have my snacks; I will not overexercise and I will be accountable to a support person about my exercise; and lastly, I will be honest with myself and with others about how I'm doing.

After fifteen years of active recovery these nonnegotiable actions remain one hundred percent relevant and are part of how I structure each day. They're a reminder of the path I must follow, and they serve as the roadmap to my success. Regardless of what's happening in my life—amid the stressors, the joys, or the routine—I can always recite these nonnegotiables in my head and return to them. I *must* return to them because they are the most immediately available and actionable directions.

Each day I recommit to recovery.

While I was working on my recovery, I was also working on regaining my life. For so long I'd been connected to the eating disorder and then I needed to be as deeply connected to recovery from it. I had to imagine and create a life individuated from the disease and this called for reflection on life before the eating disorder and then on the work I did in treatment around leading a purposeful life. As I began thinking about what I'd do next, I knew that work would somehow include children.

I'd been teaching first grade prior to entering treatment and I loved the challenges and joy that teaching brought. I knew that I found satisfaction, passion, and purpose within the classroom walls and felt that the school setting was the best place for me. A few days after moving to Denver I found a Craigslist ad for a substitute teaching job at a small nearby school. I visited and instantly loved it. There was a palpable energy exchange that occurred when I walked in the door and I knew it was the right place for me. Luckily, the head of the school agreed. Soon I filled in wherever I was needed.

This new school provided an additional support network as well as helping me refind my purpose. Being back in the school setting grounded me and being with kids inspired me to stay well. I had to be my best self so that I could show up authentically for them.

For the first time in a while, I could live not completely based around the eating disorder. I could be a teacher. I could be a young woman. I could be outdoorsy. I could be a family person. The list continued and I had limitless options without the eating disorder weighing me down. I had time and space and energy for other things that the eating disorder had crowded out. However, this new normal still meant that I needed to closely monitor my personal wellness and maintain weekly therapy. These two things were essential components of this new life—and to have the possibility of a new life felt incredible.

I still thought about food more than my friends and family without eating disorders, and I knew that I might always. I had to constantly remind myself of Dr. Wendell's words: "Recovery is not the absence of thoughts; it's the absence of behaviors." If I ate a donut in the teacher's workroom, I might think about it afterwards more than the next person—but I no longer felt the need to exercise in a compensatory manner or to restrict my intake for the remainder of the day simply because I ate that yummy donut.

The eating disorder still played a larger role in my life during this time than I had hoped—but I knew that the only way out of it was through it.

And One Day It Was Fifteen Years Later

Sometimes I look back upon this road to illness and then recovery and feel like a spectator. I know the Rachel of this story, but we share little in common today. Other days I look back and feel the pain of anorexia all over again. I think about how hard these years were and about the suffering I caused others, and it feels like almost too much to take. I can't dwell on that. Instead I move through the world now as a changed woman even though I'll always carry those moments in California and Reno with me. I no longer wear the easy-to-see physical indicators of anorexia. My weight has been normal for a decade, the lanugo covering my body has come and gone, and my hair has regained its thickness. My heart, bone density, and brain function have all returned to what was typical for me before the storm of anorexia.

My propensity toward anxiety and OCD remains, but at a level that allows freedom to move through the day in order to experience the wellness that I now know I deserve. Weekly therapy sessions with Leah continue and this continuity of care has proven essential. Exercise continues to be something that I'm very mindful of monitoring and I don't run or do long workouts at the gym. Instead, I go to yoga or Pilates, take a hike or go for a bike ride. Exercise is no longer a punishment but instead a chance to find freedom in movement and to practice gratitude for all that my body endured. Movement is now a celebration of my body's incredible resilience.

Food is nourishment and food is a joy. Food is something that I enjoy preparing and offering to others—as much as I like preparing it and offering to myself. However, food can *still* feel complicated and is *still* something that I often overthink. I know that food is to be eaten and shared and regardless of where my thinking may be, I know that my behavior and actions with food will be constant and consistent. I'm no longer hypermetabolic but I still require a high caloric intake each day to keep up with my genetics and lifestyle.

Fifteen years later and I'm still in the classroom! Here I find the answers to life's most important and pressing questions right in the minds and hearts of my students. They continue to sustain me as they offer hope for a braver, kinder, and more inclusive world. Teaching is simultaneously exhausting and restorative. It demands that I take great care of my own self, and I must practice what I preach. I must nourish my body properly, and I must rest my body and mind so I can tackle what's next.

I remain deeply devoted to my family and friends, and additionally to my husband who embraces each part of my story; past, present, and future. Nate feeds me both literally and figuratively and keeps me in check if he sees me waver. My devotion has further grown, as I am the proud mother of a beautiful five-year-old daughter and a lovely twenty-one-year-old bonus-daughter. I see such hope and wonder in their eyes and my heart beats in tune with theirs. My world changed dramatically when I became a mother, and raising daughters with Nate is my greatest joy. In moments, my parents continue to fear those siren sounds of subtraction will again come calling. However, we dare to fervently believe that this day will never come.

We know far too many who have lost this battle, and we humbly but gratefully carry on for those not able to.

Endnotes

1. Trace, S.E., Baker, J.H., Penas-Ledo, E., & Bulik, C. M. (2013). "The genetics of eating disorders." Annual Review of Clinical Psychology, 9, 589-620.

2. Ulfvebrand, S., Birgegard, A., Norring, C., Hogdahl, L., and von Housswolff, Y. (2015). "Psychiatric comorbidity in women and men with eating disorders results from a large clinical database." *Psychiatry Research*, 230(2), 294-299

3. Kaye, Walter MD, Christina E Wierenga, Ursula F. Bailey, Alan N. Simmons, Amanda Bischoff-Grethe (2013). "Nothing Tastes as Good as Anorexia Feels." *Trends in Neurosciences*. Volume 36. Issue 2: 110-120.

4. Edward Steichen Quotes. BrainyQuote.com, BrainyMedia, Inc (2025). www.brainyquote.com/quotes/edward_steichen_141183.

5. Greenblatt, James M. MD. *Answers to Anorexia*. North Branch, MN: Sunrise River Press (2010).

6. Fromm, Erich. *The Sane Society*. Rinehart and Company, Inc. (Jan 1, 1959).

Acknowledgments

This book cut to the bones of my family. Writing fiction would have suited me better but our story was all too real and demanded to be told. If it can help one person, if it can shed light on an illness that is too often stereotyped and stigmatized, and if it offers genuine hope, Rachel and I will be thrilled.

It took several villages to raise this book. Thanks to the Vermont College of Fine Arts MFA in Writing Program. Abby Frucht, Laurie Alberts, Larry Sutin, Connie May Fowler, and Sue William Silverman were the best, and often most demanding, mentors one could ask for.

Thanks to the Bread Loaf Writers' Conference and specifically to Ann Hood. Being on the "mountain" was a magical time and made my writing stand up and get to work.

Thanks to my beta readers: Catherine Buni, Melissa Cronin, Karl and Merrillyn Decker, Carol Laurenzano, Mark Levine, Betty Reed, Geeda Searfoorce, and Julie Vogel. Your commentaries kept me going!

Thanks to TRIO, my writing group, my scaffold. Every writer needs a Betty and a Julie for accountability, insight, and of course, Zoom meetings, in-person adventures, and fun.

Thanks to Hester Kaplan and Amabel Kylee Siorghlas for their fine editing eyes and generous spirits.

Thanks to my publisher, Samantha Kolber of Rootstock Publishing. You felt the raw and hard times, but also heard the laughter, in *LIGHT*.

Thanks to Mike and Rachel. You two are my everything.

And finally, endless thanks to Mark. You have faith in me even when mine falters. Your footsteps follow me up every mountain we climb and when I slip, you're there.

Bibliography for Further Reading

Arnold, Carrie. *Decoding Anorexia: How Breakthroughs in Science Offer Help for Eating Disorders.* New York, NY: Routledge, 2013.

Brown, Harriet. *Brave Girl Eating: A Family's Struggle with Anorexia.* New York: Harper Collins, 2010.

Brown, Harriet. *Body of Truth: How Science, History, and Culture Drive Our Obsession with Weight.* Boston: First Da Capo Press Edition, 2015.

Collins, Laura. *Eating with Your Anorexic: How My Child Recovered through Family-based Treatment and Yours Can Too.* New York: McGraw-Hill, 2005.

Dunkle, Clare and Elena. *Elena Vanishing: A Memoir of Anorexia.* San Francisco: Chronicle Books LLC: 2015.

Greenblatt, James M., MD. *Answers to Anorexia.* North Branch, MN: Sunrise River Press, 2010.

Hornbacher, Marya. *Wasted.* New York: HarperCollins Publishers. 1998.

Liu, Aimee. *Restoring our Bodies, Reclaiming our Lives.* Boston: Trumpeter Books, 2011.

Naidoo, Uma, MD. *This Is Your Brain On Food: An Indispensable Guide For The Surprising Foods That Fight Depression, PTSD, ADHD, Anxiety, OCD and More.* Little, Brown Spark, 2020.

Naidoo, Uma, MD. *Calm Your Mind With Food: A Revolutionary Guide to Controlling Your Anxiety.* Little, Brown Spark, 2023.

Thomas, Jennifer, J., PhD, and Jenni Schaefer. *Almost Anorexic. Is My (or My Loved One's) Relationship with Food a Problem?* Center City, MN: Hazelden Publishing, 2013.

Resources

Academy for Eating Disorders
www.aedweb.org
703.556.9222

Eating Disorder Hope: Maudsley Parents
www.eatingdisorderhope.com
866.932.1264

Families Empowered and Supporting Treatment of Eating Disorders (F.E.A.S.T)
www.feast-ed.org
855.503.3278

Manna Fund Providing limited scholarships for those seeking treatment.
www.mannafund.org
770.495.9775

National Association of Anorexia Nervosa and Associated Disorders (ANAD)
www.anad.org
847.831.3438

National Eating Disorders Association (NEDA)
www.nationaleatingdisorders.org
212.575.6200

About the Authors

Nancy Y. Levine is a former pediatric neurology nurse. She received her MFA in writing from Vermont College of Fine Arts and attended Bread Loaf Writers' Conference. Her work has appeared in *Vermont Magazine*, *Mothers and Daughters: A Poetry Collection*, and *The Sun* magazine. When not reading or writing, she can be found hiking Vermont trails with her husband and their labradoodle, lifting weights at the gym, or trying to look busy when she's actually daydreaming.

Rachel Levine-Spates received her EdM from the Harvard Graduate School of Education and is the director of student well-being and social emotional learning at St. George's Independent School in Germantown, Tennessee. Rachel also provides peer support for those suffering eating disorders. Rachel's story, "Never Healthy Enough," appeared in *Self Magazine* in April 2015. When not working, or staying a step ahead of her four-year-old daughter, she can be found couch-side watching basketball with her husband.

We Grow Our Books in Montpelier, Vermont

Learn more about our titles in Fiction, Nonfiction, Poetry and Children's Literature at the QR code below or visit www.rootstockpublishing.com.

www.ingramcontent.com/pod-product-compliance
Lightning Source LLC
Chambersburg PA
CBHW030520080526
44586CB00011B/271